The WHITBREAD
Rugby World '92

The WHITBREAD Rugby World '92

NIGEL STARMER-SMITH
AND IAN ROBERTSON

Macdonald
Queen Anne Press

A QUEEN ANNE PRESS BOOK

© Lennard Associates Ltd 1991

First published in 1991 by
Queen Anne Press, a division of
Macdonald & Co (Publishers) Ltd
165 Great Dover Street
London SE1 4YA

A member of Maxwell Macmillan Pergamon Publishing Corporation

British Cataloguing in Publication Data
The Whitbread rugby world '92.
1. Rugby football
I. Starmer-Smith, Nigel, 1944- II. Robertson, Ian, 1945-
796.33'3

ISBN 0 356 20320 4

Made by Lennard Associates Ltd
Mackerye End, Harpenden, Herts AL5 5DR

Design by Forest Publication Services
Printed and bound in England by
The Bath Press, Bath, Avon.

The publishers and authors would like to thank the
 following for their help in providing the photographs for this book:
Colin Elsey, C. Henry, Peter Bush, Ian Robertson, John Aherne,
Northampton Chronicle and Echo, Sportsfile and *The Scotsman*

CONTENTS

WHEN THE EARTH MOVED

by DUDLEY WOOD, Secretary of the RFU

I suppose that another time when the earth moved for me – I am speaking metaphorically of course – was on 16th March 1991 when a packed house at Twickenham jubilantly saw their team home against France and to the Grand Slam. It has been a momentous year with an unprecedented succession of highlights at our national ground, starting with the Barbarian Centenary Match, England's revenge against Argentina and a Varsity Match in which the tables were turned, then a glorious Five Nations Championship and on to a splendid Junior club knock-out final, a wonderful County Championship final – for Cornishmen the greatest occasion of all – a dramatic Pilkington Cup final and eventually the Middlesex Sevens finals with the favourites pipped on the post. What more could anyone ask?

Dudley Wood

Throughout the season the new North Stand has looked resplendent and has provided a preview of the stadium to come when it will be joined up with the new East and West stands, to be built to the same design. For those of us who work there, Twickenham is very special and we are anxious to see it realise its full potential as the most prestigious and best equipped rugby ground in the world.

Recognising that Twickenham cannot meet all its needs, the Rugby Football Union has recently acquired its second ground, incorporating the former pitch of Wolverhampton Wanderers Football Club, at Castlecroft in the West Midlands. A new stand enclosing four changing rooms, a fitness centre and a conference hall has been completed and Castlecroft becomes the Rugby Football Union Centre for Youth and Schools Rugby.

And so to a World Cup to which acres of space will be devoted by newspapers and hours of time on television. The game of rugby football has moved a long way since its origins.

As my old games master used to say, life is a process of discovery – about things, about places, about other people and most of all about yourself. I remember how I discovered I would never make a front row forward. It was not an important match and I was going through the usual ritual as a number 8 forward, leaning on the scrums and obstructing in the line-outs, when one of our props departed permanently for the dressing room, limping dramatically like the ham actor we all knew he was.

Our genius of a skipper, his face contorted in agony at the effort of thought, deduced that only one positional change would be needed if our number 8 forward, standing 6ft 3in in his socks, were to join the dwarfs in the front row. We would then play without a number 8 because there were no replacements allowed in those days.

My opposing prop, a squat, taciturn gorilla of indeterminate age, was seriously deficient of many of the features traditionally possessed by rugby players such as hair, teeth and a neck. He was not a pretty sight. The only time I saw him smile was when a scrum was called and I took up my position opposite him. In the next few minutes, which lasted an age, I found myself at one moment studying blades of grass at much closer proximity than I have ever seen them before and at the next suspended high in the sky watching startled clouds scudding by – and it was very painful.

When at last the scrum broke up and I stumbled thankfully away in the general direction play had taken, I became aware of my opposite number jogging comfortably along beside me. He spoke for the first time. "And how was it for you?" he remarked conversationally. It was only then I realised what he had done to me.

How do we all hope to see rugby progress into the twenty-first century? The example of other school sports is not encouraging. True, a great deal of club sport is still being played. The same will probably long be true of rugby football and it is perhaps an optimistic sign that politicians and educationalists are beginning to realize that without some form of physical activity in schools we are becoming a very unhealthy nation. Even so, the emphasis on team sports which existed in the old grammar school days is unlikely to return.

The grass-roots of the game the junior clubs will continue largely untouched by modern pressures but unless they recruit and teach the game they are bound to shrink in size and numbers. The so-called 'demographic time-bomb' will see to that. And the top, the shop window, the senior clubs, well there is a choice.

Either we are going to wring our hands and yield to the commercial pressures which require us to accept that money dictates who, when and how we play and that television and sponsorship call the tune, or else we claim the right to be what we have always been – different.

Paradoxically, the commercial route means not more money but no money, except for the few. All the evidence points to the fact that you end up with a relatively small number of clubs and performers who cream off all that is going, leaving the rest of the sport to wither and die. Association

The full RFU Committee lines up for a 'team' photo below Twickenham's new North Stand.

Football is about to take a large step in that direction, with its Premier League but the ultimate scenario is that of American Football with its mega-buck hype and virtually no grass-roots at all. In fact the growth of rugby union football in the States is said to be a reaction against the professionalism of American Football.

Rugby Football has always been different – elitist yet classless. Your 'greats' mingle happily with your 'also rans'. Yet everyone who is part of the game realises sooner or later that it is a sporting freemasonry and a privilege to be a member. To succumb to the commercial pressures which seek to divide us would be a tragedy. Club committees should reflect on the purpose of their sport when considering fixtures, competitions and sponsorship and not be led stray by the 'money men'.

CARLING IN CONVERSATION
with NIGEL STARMER-SMITH

N.C.S-S: Will, it must be very difficult as England's rugby captain to have anything resembling a normal working life?

W.D.C.C: It is difficult, especially when the Five Nations Championship is on. That's a two-month period of great intensity and on top of the playing side there are the captaincy responsibilities relating to an unending round of media demands. And then there is the need to maintain contact with players at all times, discussing matters with all members of the squad, building up to the next game. One game over, maybe a couple of days relaxing, and then you're into the next one. Its basically a lot of work.

N.C.S-S: With your style of leadership I sense that your captaincy role is more important off the field than on it. What do you discuss with the players between games?

W.D.C.C: I do take the off-field side to captaincy very seriously and, yes, I do think it is the more significant. I've always been amazed at the attitude of those who feel their captaincy duties don't really start until you meet up at the hotel a couple of days before the match. I think it's all about making sure that you talk to players before they arrive, so that they have a feel for what it is you want to try to attempt to do and the tone you want to set. That way it's much easier to keep it going right through to the game. The players have been able to think ahead and concentrate on what's expected, what's required and their individual responsibilities.

Will Carling, the motivator on the field and in business.

N.C.S-S: Is this approach something you have developed yourself, because it's seldom been the case that an international captain has been almost a 'welfare' figure, concerning himself with each individual in the build-up to the match, talking to players who have been chosen, dropped or not selected at all? Communication, or at least a lack of it, was something that till recently was a familiar grouse with the players.

W.D.C.C: I think Geoff Cooke has been very, very influential in opening up the communication channels with players. But to me as a young captain when I came in – and still pretty young in this context – I think my duty, and my wish, was to involve the senior players as much as possible, to make them feel more responsible for what we, as a team, were doing. Responsible for how we were playing, how we were training, and so on. That was really the way I saw it when I started out. I think I talked to them more to get their ideas, rather than trying to feed my thoughts to them. The likes of Wade Dooley, Rory Underwood, Peter Winterbottom had more than 40 caps apiece; that is remarkable experience, and you would be crazy not to make use of it.

N.C.S-S: But was there any resentment from the senior players that you should come in as captain at just 22 and take over the side when some of them had been there since the start of the Eighties?

W.D.C.C: I think that very fact is why I have so much respect for them all, because no-one ever showed any resentment to me. It's human nature that some of them must have been disappointed and have thought, "What about me?", but no-one every said a thing. That's something for which I have always been grateful. I have always had tremendous support, with no unpleasant or uncomfortable situations on that account.

N.C.S-S: You've explained your commitment as captain so let me repeat the opening question. How can you possibly sustain, let alone concentrate upon, a career?

W.D.C.C: It's very hard. I might spend the best part of a day, several times in a period of a few weeks, putting together some clips of action from earlier matches - we call them 'horror movies' - of moments in a game where things went wrong. Luckily I have facilities to compile videos as part of my business life; an example of how fortunate it is my rugby responsibilities go very much hand in glove with my own career interests which run along the same channels in motivation and management. I look back to when I used to work as an executive trainee for Mobil and I cannot see that the way I view captaincy was compatible with holding down a normal office job. The rugby element now takes up so much time that I can easily spend a morning on the phone talking to players about how we should organize our defence. Three or four players, a chat with Geoff, and the morning's gone - and that is when I'm meant to be working!

N.C.S-S: You prompt the question then, as to whether your changes in career direction - first of all pursuing an army career in your father's footsteps, then switching to executive trainee with an oil company, and now as a self-employed person - were a direct response to the fact that it is no longer possible to play rugby for England, become captain in your style, and be a full-time employee?

W.D.C.C: I think I would find it very hard, if not impossible. That being said, what I now do is something which had always been a career ambition, but it certainly helps me that I can decide for myself when and where I train, when I work and when I play. If I were still working for Mobil I am sure I would always feel that I was not doing a good enough job for them. In the back of your mind there had to be a niggling doubt and a guilt, that the rest of the graduate trainees were working as hard as they could whilst you were taking off x number of weeks in a year.

N.C.S-S: Now you have your own company, Inspiration Horizons, did you see your rugby fame, if not yet fortune, being a key element in persuading to set up on your own?

Will Carling, with Geoff Cooke and Roger Uttley, at the annual RFU Golf Tournament at Effingham Golf Club.

W.D.C.C: Yes, it has been significant and people are quick to suggest that my rugby notoriety was the only motivating factor. Not true. It is an area in which I have always wanted to work. I read psychology at Durham, and I have always been fascinated by what motivates people, how to lead people, how to manage people, so I was lucky with the rugby and the fact that my England captaincy took me directly into this same area of interest. It was never a case of "let's think about what I can do now".

N.C.S-S: So, more precisely, what does your company set out to provide?

W.D.C.C: Quite simply, trying to relate the lessons learned in sport by top sportsmen to business. Top sportsmen set themselves goals, personal goals, and plan and prepare how they are going to achieve those objectives. From studying athletes you learn lessons which are of great validity for business. Businesses are made up of teams, teams need to be motivated, led and managed. There is a close parallel, and a great deal that can be translated from sport to business, and vice-versa. I hope to be able to provide a service and ideas for companies.

Will Carling and Wayne Shelford make guest appearances at the announcement of a World Cup sponsor.

N.C.S-S: So much has been written, said and discussed of late on the regulations relating to amateurism in rugby. How do these apply to your business and your own promotional activities?

W.D.C.C: There is a tremendous grey area, it seems. As far as my business is concerned, quite simply it is a business. I can't promote myself or my company maybe as much as I would like to because I might be accused of flouting the rules. But this is a business, a serious business, and, as I say, something I have wanted to do for many, many years. I do find it a bit galling occasionally to be told I can't do certain things when in fact it is part of my full time job.

N.C.S-S: Although matters may have moved on by the time this interview is published, currently few people on either side of the fence, seem at all clear as to what activities players may or may not indulge in for financial reward?

W.D.C.C: I think that is the nub of the problem. Nothing as yet is crystal clear. Until it is, there will inevitably be a lot of friction. I see it as a waste for the game and, as the Grand Slam season has shown, it is doing the image of the game no good at all. I think everyone should take a deep breath and look at the position constructively, accept the fact that times have changed and, most importantly, decide how we can best promote the game, promote the players, and encourage more youngsters to get involved.

N.C.S-S: Do you, at the end of the 1991 season, feel that the players are being exploited with so much money in the game of rugby and little of it finding its way to the players?

W.D.C.C: Yes. Not a lot of it is coming to the players. The prospect of financial gain is not what motivates the players. We do not play for England and contemplate the thousands of pounds that might come to us as a result; but why can't we have our cut? Certain players have now become publicly-known figures and people are interested in them. I feel, therefore, that allowing these players to receive financial reward as a consequence of their fame will not cause any harm; conversely using these players as promotional vehicles for the game can only serve rugby's best interests. I think also that, if the administrators accept that you can now market players, the game's profile is going to improve dramatically. Youngsters are going to want to play like Jerry Guscott, Rob Andrew or Wade Dooley, and relating to these 'star' players will encourage them to play rugby. That to me is the crucial thing, not "Oh dear! There's money in the game", but "There is money in the game, how can we use it and the players for the good of the game?"

N.C.S-S: Do the players see an inevitable progression towards being paid for playing, ultimately, a professional game?

W.D.C.C: It's hard to say. I suppose if you asked people four years ago if the subsequent changes would have come about they would have denied the likelihood. I now find it difficult to forecast the changes that might happen over the next four years. But you know and I know that there is something special about rugby and that is one thing the players want to keep alive. Even fiercely competitive international teams will spend the evening after a game together, at the same meal, the same party, having fun together. That unique character and appeal is something the players want to keep and, despite what anyone may think, they are trying very hard to ensure that this element does remain. The sociability and fun that rugby engenders is sacrosanct. What will happen in terms of paying players, I don't know. I can't predict that. I know that administrators should respect the fact that players want to keep what attracts them to the game - the great friendships that can be made and kept.

N.C.S-S: But do the international players of the moment *want* to be paid?

W.D.C.C: I can only speak for the England squad, and their answer is no. We don't think we should be paid £5,000 an international, or whatever. What we want is to be able to benefit, like some other countries now, from off-the-field activities. Anything off-the-field seems to me to be a perfectly legitimate area of activity from which to benefit. But no, I don't want to be paid for playing, nor, as far as I am aware, does any other member of the England squad.

N.C.S-S: Do you think, though, that the time has come when the commitment required is too great to maintain rugby as an amateur game - squad weekends, match weekends, tours, maybe 90 days given over to rugby in a year?

W.D.C.C: It is clearly getting far harder now for companies, especially in the present economic climate, to give players the amount of time off they require. I think that when a league structure is put on an amateur game, once vast commercial interests are brought into a game by the administrators themselves, you are certain to find it very hard to keep a game amateur. The public and supporters want always to see England play better, to go on improving. To achieve that the players must inevitably spend more time training, spend more time on skills, spend more time as a team unit. Equally important to the players is that it is getting harder and harder for them to compete in their everyday jobs with fellow employees who can spend much more time on building their careers.

N.C.S-S: And here you are, putting together tapes for the next team gathering, discussing rugby with me, then no doubt phoning, or being phoned, on rugby related matters, followed by a training session at the gym - is that anything short of a 'professional' sporting life?

W.D.C.C: No, you are right. I think the burden on the England squad in the international season (which is getting ever closer to 12 months a year!) is that we are trying to do as much training as we can. That probably involves training every day, as well as work, as well as trying to carry on some semblance of a social (or family) life. It is getting extremely hard, and I think players will now burn out a lot quicker than they used to.

N.C.S-S: What about the additional pressures of captaincy? Basically, you have to be 'on top'; available, it seems, to everyone.

W.D.C.C: You have to accept it. I love the captaincy role and get a lot of satisfaction out of it. The interviews that come from all quarters are part, I feel, of the captain's job. You have a responsibility to talk to the media. There are pressures which I do find hard, but at the end of the day there are so many benefits that it would be petty indeed to carp about the few things that irritate.

N.C.S-S: But captaincy was not a familiar role when you were appointed as leader, plucked from England's playing strength almost out of the blue.

W.D.C.C: No. To find my previous experience of captaincy at any level you have to go back to England Schoolboys. Geoff obviously saw something he wanted, but it came out of nowhere really, and I was only too happy to give it a go. Yes, it came as a shock – a nice one though. You always have a dream, and mine was that one day I might captain England. When it came at the age of 22 I could scarce believe it. Now I've been lucky enough to do it and the thrill and sense of honour is something I could never put into words. A dream of mine and a childhood ambition fulfilled.

A captain still has to train.

BAN THE GOAL-KICKERS!
by MICK CLEARY

No sooner had Simon Hodgkinson's boot stopped swinging on its record-breaking season than another size ten was being swung with equal venom from the other direction. Stamped indelibly on its toe-cap was the message – 'Ban the goal-kickers'.

It happens every time that a goal-kicker comes to the fore. New Zealand's Don Clarke got the treatment; Dusty Hare had a dose of it and now Hodgkinson. It's not as if it's just an aggrieved opposition putting the boot in. There would be a measure of validity in Welshmen, bemoaning the unjustness of their record defeat by England in Cardiff, this year attributable, as it was, almost entirely to the world record seven penalty goals struck by the Nottingham full back.

No, the Welsh kept quiet. (So too did the English, but that's another story). In fact there weren't too many cauliflower-eared types on the bandwagon which trundled through the season asking for major changes to the laws in order to keep Hodgkinson's feet firmly on the ground. The outcry was led by the bar-stool pundits. Those who tune in to the game for two or three matches a year and then proceed to hold forth on what they have seen as if they were seasoned experts.

Mind you they were right in describing the Wales-England game as a bore. It was. But not because Simon Hodgkinson kicked seven penalties. It was a poor game because of the number of mistakes made, the number of wrong options taken and the flawed skills displayed. Of course many of those mistakes led to an infringement which was then severely punished by the England full back.

The critics who called for more open, adventurous, throw-caution-to-the-winds rugby as a result of their analysis of this match miss the point entirely. Certainly argue that the differential between try and penalty should be altered slightly; certainly argue that the offences for which a penalty rather than a free kick should be given be restricted still further. But do not argue that kicking is boring. It is anything but.

Kicking for goal is highly theatrical. Indeed it is a play in itself. The infringement, the referee's whistle, the deliberation over whether to run or kick, the teeing-up, the slow walk back, the crowd's anticipation of success or failure, the shuffle towards the ball and over it goes. Or doesn't.

Michael Lynagh, who passed 600 international points at the Sydney Football Stadium in July 1991.

A bit of body language helps this goal attempt by Dusty Hare.

Remember Don Fox at the rugby league final, final seconds, conversion in front of the posts to win the Challenge Cup and what happens? He misses. Was that dramatic or was it not? Would we still be living through the man's agonies again every year as the sequence is replayed if it weren't. Jack van der Schyff, the Springbok full back, has lived through the same nightmare. In 1955 Schyff had a kick that would have given South Africa victory over the British Isles, 24-23. Legend has it that so trustworthy was the Schyff boot that the scoreboard operator had actually removed the 22 in anticipation of the kick being successful. Schyff did not play for the Springboks again.

Another country, another sport – American Football. Hollywood script-writers could not have penned a more riveting finale. Buffalo Bills against the New York Giants, a global audience of over 100 million and it's all down to a kick. Scott Norwood had had nothing else to do all season, nay, all his life, but to prepare for this moment. Two weeks earlier he had taken his side through to the Superbowl courtesy of a last minute conversion. Could he do it this time? The range was one yard further than he'd ever managed: the tension was strangling most of his team-mates who could not bear to watch. They made the right choice. He missed. That was no anti-climax: it was just the opposite. All life condensed into the few brief seconds which it took to fire the ball through the air.

The miss can then be as tantalisingly exciting as the success. Even though that emotion is heightened in direct ratio to the simplicity of the kick, there can be no justification for agreeing with a recent innovation of the Scottish Rugby Union. For a trial period in certain matches at the start of this coming season, all conversions will be taken in front of goal. Why, I have no idea. What's the point of having a scoring opportunity which is 99% certain to succeed. It's often been pointed out that there is some sort of discrepancy in a game which offers a greater reward for a forward rumble over line between the posts than a classic three-quarter score which ends with a try in the corner. If you wanted to be truly meritorious, then you might reverse the positioning of the conversions, with the try in the corner having a kick in front of the posts and vice-versa. The suggestion is almost as nonsensical as the Scottish proposal. The reason is simple. Scoring should be difficult, not easy. The joy of witnessing a kick sail over from the touchline is far greater than seeing it dabbed over from in front of the posts.

And so to another misconception. Running games are better

than kicking games. Nonsense. There is just no reason to side with the premise that the more you see people run and the less you see them kick, the better the match you are watching. Some of the most tedious matches I have seen have been high-scoring, candy-floss displays where the tackling has been non-existent. The tries scored have been meaningless, having neither the virtue of graft nor inspiration behind them. Of course, games like the World Cup thriller between France and Australia, or the 37-21 Five Nations between Scotland and Ireland in 1989 have been classics in their own right. It just happened to fall that way on the day. Conversely some of the most engaging games I've ever seen have ended 3-0. If the quality of the play is riveting, be it between the forwards or the backs, then there can be no grumbling. What do people want – basketball, a sport in which a score is guaranteed on virtually every attack and which has no real dramatic virtues until the closing moments?

Paul Thorburn's record points tally for Wales was not enough to prevent the decline in their international status.

It has been argued that watching England grind their way to the Grand Slam last season was, at times, a painful process. Well, the atmosphere at Twickenham on that final Saturday did not seem too down-beat to me. Even if one accepts a measure of justification in criticising England's methods, then there can be no doubt that it was that forward supremacy which indirectly produced one of the greatest tries ever seen. Would France have had the need to run the ball from way behind the posts if they thought there was a reasonable chance of scoring more conventionally? England's power up front and the constant threat of the Hodgkinson boot forced France to cut loose as only they can. There would not have been half as much pleasure in witnessing that score if tries were being run in by both sides with carefree abandon. The beauty was in the contrast of styles. If one side is dominating through the pack and the boot it is up to the other side to counter that. Alter the game by tinkering with the laws and you risk losing the fascination of that duel.

Grant Fox, whose reliability has frequently been a great boost to New Zealand's morale.

Of course no-one likes to watch a stop-start game. In a cup match I saw last season the whistle was blown 55 times for either a free kick or a penalty. Add in a few scrums and line-outs and you can easily appreciate that there wasn't a lot else to see. The referee has a huge role to play in determining just what type of match evolves. Clive Norling has been known not to award a single penalty in a game. But, and a large but it is, he can only do that with the willing support of the players. If they are determined to cheat, then he will award a penalty. As he says: "There can be no two ways about it: the cheats must be punished".

In a nutshell, that is why the kickers should be applauded not derided. They keep the game honest. As Dusty Hare points out: "There's so much cheating going on already, that if you reduce the punishment for an offence even more then the game will become even more cramped. The good goalkickers can help to create a better spectacle not reduce it. If a side knows that the offside law is going to be properly enforced and that a bloke with the deadly accuracy of Hodgkinson is on the other side, then they will stay back. Offside is what makes the game so tight: threequarters coming up on their opposite number too quickly. The French are superb at it: they go so quickly and all at the same pace, that it's almost impossible to spot. In a club match, one of the guys will invariably be a bit faster than the others and so the offside can be spotted a bit more easily. If you limit the power of the kickers then you will ruin the game."

Such is the consistency of the current crop of international goal-kickers – Hodgkinson, Lynagh and Fox – that it's easy to take for granted what you are witnessing. In many ways the goal kicker is the most accomplished player on the field. No other player will spend as much time honing his particular skill. No other players has to cope with the huge pressure that a goal-kicker faces.

"All the great kickers have to practise far more seriously than I did," says Hare. "Their precision on the day reflects that. It's not that more penalties are being awarded in games; it's that the boys are getting a higher ratio of success. Two other things have changed since my day. One, the ball is much better; two, the grounds are much better. We were still using the old leather thing when I first started which would get like a lump of concrete in the rain. The difficulty of kicking that any distance was made worse by the state of some of the international grounds. A few days of rain and the pitch would soon cut up. All the venues now seem so much better and the players have taken full advantage."

Simon Hodgkinson lost his international place in Australia, despite his record total in England's Grand Slam.

In all probability the International Board will accept a proposal to increase the try to five points. Fair enough: we all love to see tries scored and if the new system of scoring encourages a side to run the ball rather than kick to touch fair enough. But the danger is that sides may soon reckon that, in order to stop five points being scored, it might be worth the risk of conceding three. Players will always find a way round the laws. Keeping the cheats on the straight and narrow is the great value of the goal-kickers.

ON THE HOME FRONT

THE CLUB ADMINISTRATOR
by BARRIE CORLESS, Northampton RFC

Competitive club rugby in the form of league and cup competitions is here with a vengeance. The latest message from the senior clubs is that they want more still, so the impact will be even greater. There is no doubt in my mind

that such competition has on the whole been good for the game. I accept the fact that the loss of many traditional Anglo-Welsh fixtures is very sad, both from a playing and spectating point of view, and for the variety they give to a club's fixture list. Perhaps other ways of maintaining many of these long-standing traditional fixtures has to be found. On the other hand, the competitiveness of the England XV is no accident. Players are on the whole fitter than ever before and the extra edge gained through league rugby has seen England victorious in some tense, closely-fought games.

Barrie Corless –
from player to
administrator.

Club's are generally more ambitious now than they were in the past – some to maintain their status in Division 1 of the National Leagues, some to regain the stature of former golden years and some because of the opportunity to have a crack at illustrious neighbours, previously denied them by a fixture system based on tradition rather than merit. As the pressure on players increases, so do our expectations of the club in terms of the players' package. By this I do not mean financial rewards; reimbursement for out of pocket expenses travel expenses yes, but I also mean the provision of top class playing and training facilities, the preparation of individual fitness and player development programmes and the provision of the best in medical back-up for a start. In other words, the club provides the environment in which their players can best enjoy their rugby and perform to their full potential.

This has led to a handful of clubs taking the forward-thinking step of employing an individual, full-time, to take on various roles within the club. The demands of club administration are now such that it becomes extremely difficult to satisfy them on a part-time voluntary basis. Before this step is taken, however, it is absolutely essential that the club is united behind the decision and gives full support to the employee. If the appointment of a full-time administrator doesn't bring about the desired effect, or at least not as quickly as anticipated, it is all too easy to pass the blame to the employee rather than examining the system within which he works. Clubs must be clear in their own mind of the role the club administrator will perform and of the type of person they want. A precise job description should be produced. A chain of command should be outlined to speed up communication in both directions. This should be supportive and constructive rather than one that interferes. Here at Northampton no honorary positions have been lost due to my appointment. The biggest asset the club has is access to my time to carry out many of the day to day functions of the club, hopefully more efficiently than previously.

Do not make the mistake of asking the club administrator to be 'all things to all men'. Running the playing side of the club and satisfying the players' demands both on and off the field is very time consuming if done properly. It is dangerous to couple this with responsibility for commercial, social and other fund raising activities within the club as well. The costs of running a senior club are enormous and revenue generated has to be maximised in order to cover these outgoings. This again is a full-time job if the full potential of the club is to be realised.

Let me now be rather more specific about my role at Northampton. Historically the club had a reputation to rank with any in England, with a veritable 'Who's Who' of international rugby on the honours board. However, several years of mismanagement and neglect had seen the Saints slip to the foot of Division 2 of the Courage National Leagues. At a recent AGM, a group of forward-thinking individuals persuaded the membership that the time was right for a change if the club wasn't to slip even further. The membership overwhelmingly voted in support and the new committee have repaid their faith many times over. It was shortly after this AGM that my appointment was confirmed with the simple but challenging brief of a) attaining Division 1 status and then b) maintaining a challenge at the top of Division 1. To move from the bottom of Division 2 to Division 1 and the Pilkington Cup final in three years does not happen by accident, nor is it the work of one man. Initially the players, coaches and committee set out their aims. Membership grew and gradually the commercial side improved. Many off-the-field improvements were made, updating the floodlights, building a permanent TV platform and eight hospitality boxes. A new match sponsor's suite is also nearing completion. New lights were erected on the training pitch and extensive pitch drainage undertaken at Franklin's Gardens.

On the playing side, recruitment centred initially around the student sector, while other new members had moved into the area through employment opportunities. More direction was given to the players in terms of patterns of play and individual and unit responsibilities. Programmes were drawn up and players fitness monitored. Individual development programmes were instigated.

Young players were given the opportunity of 1st XV rugby at the expense of older players nearing the end of their playing days. These ambitious young men soon captured the imagination of the supporters and, perhaps motivated by the committee's effort to build a Division 1 set-up, gained promotion and reached the Pilkington Cup semi-final within two years.

I expanded my role to that of improving links with the many junior clubs in the area, to try and give a boost to schools rugby in the county. I have always believed that the senior club in the area should set the standards as a rugby centre of excellence. This we have done by:

Northampton's inspiration on the field – Wayne Shelford (left) and captain Gary Pearce (right) with highly-promising young prop Gavin Baldwin.

1. Keeping our neighbours fully informed as to changes in policy at Northampton which will impact on them, for example, by changing our 3rd XV, formerly a mixture of social rugby players and promising ex-Colts into a flourishing Under-21 side. This will encourage many of our players to return to their former clubs, either to finish their playing days passing on the benefits of their senior club experience or, in the case of the younger players, to continue their development at a junior level before returning as a more mature and experienced player at some stage in the future.

2. Running a series of roadshows around the county in conjunction with junior clubs and the local education authority, the idea being to increase the

number of young people playing the game and to encourage non-rugby-playing schools to take up rugby football.

3. Running a centre of excellence for players of known ability in conjunction with the county schools committee. Under 14, Under 15, Under 16 and Under 18 groups have trained regularly at Franklin Gardens with the assistance of Saints coaches and players.

For a club like Northampton to sustain its current progress it needs a strong club/school infrastructure in order to develop players of sufficient quality. If the schools are strong, if our junior clubs are strong, Northampton will be strong and that is our aim.

CORNISH PRIDE

by W J BISHOP JP, President of Cornwall RFU
and for 16 years Cornwall Representative in the RFU Committee

The County Championship is by far the oldest competition in English Rugby and was first played on a knockout basis in 1890-91. Four Divisions were formed, North-East, North-West, South-East, South-West. Cornwall first entered the Championship in season 1892-93.

Cornwall have the honour of celebrating Centenary Year as Champions, having only won it once before in 1908 in a match played at Redruth against Durham, winning by 17 points to 3.

That match became part of Cornish folklore and all would-be young rugby players were raised on a diet of black and gold nostalgia, the greatest achievement in Cornish rugby, only surpassed in the past season.

Several of those Cornish players of 1908 gained international caps, but even before that the whole of the side were singularly honoured. As the county champions, they were invited to represent England in the 1908 Olympic Games at the White City. In the final, Cornwall representing England, were beaten by Australia and the Cornwall players were each presented with an Olympic cap of red and white plus one silver medal, which is still on show in the St Ives clubhouse.

Generations of Cornish players have had a lot to live up to with an eager army of supporters seeking success and looking for new heroes to match that early success.

In 1989 hopes were high. Cornwall had reached Twickenham for the first time in a final and who were the opposition? Durham. Would history repeat itself? Trelawny's Army left the Duchy in their thousands to cheer on their team, but it was not to be. Cornwall lost in the closing minutes, and, although a great day was had by all, they returned empty-handed.

Result apart, it was a good day for rugby - brilliant weather, the largest crowd to date for a county final at Twickenham, and the pleasure of having the Patron of Cornwall, the Duke of Edinburgh, to make it a royal occasion.

It was against this background of two matches spanning nearly a hundred years that, in 1991, Cornwall beat Warwickshire at Redruth in the semi-final to set up what was described as a dream final at Twickenham against Yorkshire on April 20th.

There has never been a build-up like it. The whole county was unified with one purpose, to be at Twickenham and see Cornwall win. All available

Referee Roger Quittenton is well placed to signal Tommy Bassett's try for Cornwall in the County Championship final.

coaches were booked, two special trains arranged, an aircraft chartered and hundreds of cars set off on the A30 to London. Cornwall RFU organised a PO Box number for ticket sales which, apart from other sources, succeeded in selling over 25,000 tickets amounting to some £220,000 in value, well illustrating the level of support in Cornwall for their team and the County Championship.

Photographs of the final clearly show the thousands of black and gold shirts, sweaters, scarves, caps, etc., that were sold, and not to any particular age group, for it was a truly a family occasion. If we thought we did well in 1989, when the last one over the bridge turned the lights out, we did even better this time.

We had the ceremonial pasty taken on a tour of the pitch and, for the first time at Twickenham, the Falmouth Marine Band, not renowned for their melody. In fact musicians are not eligible for the band, but its members are second to none in their ability to generate good fun and a great atmosphere – more important, the players love them.

Once again the Patron, Prince Philip, accepted an invitation through the Lord Lieutenant of Cornwall, Lord Falmouth, to be a royal guest and to present the trophy to the winners.

So the stage was set for the players. Only they could make it another milestone in the history of Cornish or Yorkshire rugby, and with their illustrious backgrounds both teams were keenly aware of this.

Cornwall were well prepared. Starting with a pre-season tour to Germany, fitness and preparation had been the key from the outset, and fitness was going to be of vital importance before the day was out.

The match was an amazing contest, leading 16-3 with only 16 minutes of normal time left, Yorkshire must have regarded themselves as home and dry. The Cornish team had not done well, neither for themselves nor for their 30,000 supporters. What was the turning point? Pride, passion, the realisation that they had been given the platform they wanted and hadn't played as well as they could do? Who really knows. The converted try by the Yorkshire scrum-half, which followed confusion over a kick at goal or a tapped penalty, triggered off an amazing fight back.. A converted try, a penalty and a last-minute try levelled the scores with the Cornish pack running ragged the tiring Yorkshire forwards.

In extra time there was never any doubt, for Cornwall and their supporters, there could only be one result, they had come back from the brink of defeat, a fairytale ending was in sight. Cornwall scored another 13 points to 4 by Yorkshire and so took their place in Cornish history alongside the heroes of 1908.

The euphoria continues, celebrations, dinners, a reception at County Hall, and why not, it has been a long time coming and the players have earned praise and respect. But where now for Cornish rugby? What goals to set other than to retain the title? It is hard to imagine another day like the last, but who knows?

What of Cornish club rugby? For the first time Cornwall have a senior club in the National Divisions. Redruth have gained promotion to National Division 3 of the Courage Leagues so the Cornish challenge is there on a national platform, both at County and Club level. Camborne are still in National Division Four South and with local rivalry as it is will be chasing hard on the heels of Redruth to gain promotion. They will not wish the gap to widen too far.

Rugby in the Duchy is not just a game, it is a way of life, for the future as in the past our players loyalties and route to the top are clearly defined, club - county - country, long may it continue.

The Duke of Edinburgh looks on as skipper Grant Champion salutes the Cornish army and Adrian Bick shows off the trophy.

THE TOWCESTRIANS STORY
by ROBIN GRIFFIN

On a wet and windy September evening in 1987 the first seeds of what was to be a remarkable success story were being sown on the training field of a small junior club. English rugby had just introduced the Courage National Leagues with divisions established across the country at all levels. For the first time in the game's history, clubs were about to be judged by their performance on the field and the implications of this were still to be fully grasped by many.

Towcestrians Rugby Club, based in the small country town of Towcester, with a population of 7,000 and better known for its racecourse, had for many years enjoyed success locally in the East Midlands. Indeed over the years a number of Towcestrian players had gone on to play senior rugby with Northampton and in so doing satisfied their ambition. The introduction of league rugby was about to change this traditional outlook.

On that September evening, just four days before the club was to play its first league game, as club coach I was outlining the importance of league rugby to a sceptical group of players. The text of that talk is now largely forgotten, but the theme of what was discussed is as pertinent today as it was then. Two key points formed the central thrust of the discussion. Firstly opportunity: league rugby represented opportunity for the individual to be a part of recognised success. It represented opportunity for the club to develop and to grow. The players began to identify with the theme of opportunity, particularly when related to a quote from the seventh century Muslim prophet Omar Ibu Al Halif, who said:

Four things come not back: the spoken word, the spent arrow,
time passed and neglected opportunity.

The second key point to be reinforced over and over again concerned the development of an attitude devoted to winning. The players readily embraced this winning attitude and at that very first team meeting the quote 'Winners make it happen, losers let it happen' became a part of the club's philosophy and approach.

Four seasons later with three successive league titles behind them, the best playing record of any club in the Courage Leagues – 37 wins, 1 draw and only 2 defeats – Towcestrians Rugby Club are poised to start the 1991-92 season in National Division Four (North). The club began its league life in the East Midlands-Leicester League and after losing its second league game went on to win the remainder but finished runners-up on points difference. With only one club promoted, Towcestrians made no mistake the next season, winning the league with ten straight wins. Into Midlands Division 2 (East) and another ten straight wins made them champions again gaining promotion to Midlands Division 1. With the cynics forecasting a difficult time ahead, and after a defeat by Newark and a draw at Mansfield in their opening games, it looked as if the success was to be halted. But nobody had reckoned with the spirit, determination and winning attitude created over the previous three seasons. The next eight league games were all won and, for the third season in succession, Towcestrians were promoted as winners of their league.

In any analysis of successful clubs many factors will be considered, including use of resources, improvement of facilities, school and youth development policies and of course the playing record. In the case of Towcestrians, their achievements on the field of play have provided the strongest foundation on which to build. With limited resources, with no more than adequate facilities and with a further fifteen junior clubs within a radius of ten miles all chasing local players, why have Towcestrians Rugby Club been so successful and is there a blueprint for success for other clubs?

Clearly there is a key which can unlock the doors that lead to success and in the case of Towcestrians this success was the result of many differing factors all being carefully blended together to produce the final satisfactory result. It all began with a vision, and, like Martin Luther King in 1963, a group of like minded people had a dream of what might be achieved with a degree of dedication and hard work. The opportunity was there to be taken, but where to begin and how to develop? So many questions and not many answers in those early days.

However, like many great achievements, it was not one single factor that was to be the key but many small, and on their own, insignificant actions that together produced the explosion of success. The 'vision' was turned into a highly detailed five year plan aimed at putting the club into the National leagues by 1992. This highly ambitious plan identified five key areas and in the introduction firmly stated that: "The achievement of our plans will depend upon the time

Towcestrians fly-half and captain Nigel Preece gathers the ball during match against Westleigh at Leicester which clinched the Midlands Division 1 championship.

and commitment members and others are prepared to give to the club to ensure the club's future. This will require people to take on much greater responsibility than previously, coupled with recognition of the urgency required and the trust placed in them."

The five key areas identified were as follows:–

1. **Player Recruitment** – to identify the playing strength required to elevate the club to the National leagues and actively recruit players to fulfil this goal.

2. **School and Industry Liaison** – to establish close links with schools and local industry thereby compensating for the diminishing role of rugby football in schools and enhancing the position of the club in the local community.

3. **Coaching Structure** – to co-ordinate and implement a coaching structure that is both consistent and progressive throughout the club.

4. **Management-Administration** – to create a system of management and organisation throughout the club and to co-ordinate with other club functions.

5. **Sponsorship-Finance** – to promote and obtain sponsorship for the club whilst working within agreed budgets and targets.

For each of these five key areas up to twenty-four actions and duties for each were established. Each area was headed up by a senior person, who in turn appointed his own working sub-committee.

Plans and bold statements on paper do not on their own achieve results, and it is in this area that the club has achieved so much. Results are achieved by people, and through the efforts of individuals prepared to work towards a clearly defined goal. Much of this activity and effort is of course duplicated in many clubs across the country, but perhaps Towcestrians have the edge in their development of the playing side. Success on the field has created an urgency to find resources for the improvement of both ground and clubhouse. This has been achieved through sponsorship and the successful promotion of the club to both local industry and the town itself. Without question, unless playing success had been achieved much of the associated developments would not have happened.

Undoubtedly the prime mover in achieving success has been the incredible attention to detail in the preparation of the 1st XV. Personal targets for each player are agreed, with advice on how to achieve these goals. These are then turned into targets for the team and plans produced showing how these targets can be achieved. The training and coaching programme for the whole season is laid out, showing details of all preparation, peaks required and the level of effort needed. From these pre-season discussions a pattern of play is established and training and coaching is geared to this style. To support the players in their ambitions a players' handbook has been produced each season entitled *In Pursuit of Excellence*. This 34 page booklet outlines the standards required both on and off the field in terms of dress, discipline and general behaviour. It contains details on playing patterns, positional play and organization codes, as well advice on injury treatment, pre-match eating and mental preparation.

Creating a high profile for the club and its players has encouraged players to respond with a positive attitude at training sessions and on match days. The provision of tracksuits, shell suits for travelling, and other training and playing kits has helped in the identification of the team. The continued search for publicity through press releases, letters to the press and other associated methods has assisted the club in maintaining its high profile and of course helping to attract sponsorship and new players.

The impressive backstage organisation is a further example of the attention to detail with nothing left to chance. The coaching staff ensure that every avenue is fully explored prior to important games, from watching and compiling information on the opposition and meticulous team preparation sessions through to inspecting away grounds and checking weather forecasts.

Throughout the season high levels of motivation are used, many taken from business practices. Examples of this type of motivation are the creation of a simple slogan for the season. Last season the club adopted and related to the phrase 'Winning starts on Monday'. Other typical motivational aids used include a series of famous quotes on winning which were reprinted and issued to players, the use before games of video highlights of famous matches, inspirational music and personal letters written to individual players.

TOWCESTRIANS
stand ready at the brink
Winning Starts
On Monday

"Winning starts on Monday, not 10 minutes before the game. It's confidence all week long, and it's confidence for the month before that, and the year before that. People can't get motivated on a five minute speech before they run out on the football paddock. It's something you have to wake up with — knowing that your preparation was right. Having the confidence that whatever comes up you are ready."

Winning~at Football

All of these many and varied methods of preparing and motivating the team have proved highly successful in raising the players' awareness and in maximising their playing performance.

The continued search for new ideas from such varied sports as Australian Rugby League, American Football and others has helped the club keep ahead with new and innovative ideas for preparing both the individual and the team. However, the one final missing ingredient to add to all of this is the tremendous hard work put in week in and week out by players, coaches and physiotherapy staff. Without this continuous reinforcement of skills, fitness and good habits, the other areas would be unproductive.

A new challenge lies ahead in National Division Four. The club is already deeply committed to further success and is prepared to pay the price in terms of commitment.

STUDENTS PREPARE FOR ITALY
by HARRY TOWNSEND

Michel Bonfils, a non-rugby man, should be the name on the lips of every student rugby player: for it was he who bludgeoned his way through every obstacle to make the first Students World Cup in France such a success in 1988 and pave the way for the second tournament in Italy in 1992.

Like most tournaments, the first celebration had a festival atmosphere, with Pool matches hosted by small French towns and teams taken to the hearts of local communities. Indeed, the villagers of Tautavel even brandished banners written in Russian as they followed the USSR team through dramatic victories over New Zealand, 9-3, and England, 18-16, before crashing to France 47-18 in the third and fourth place play-off.

Russia and tournament runners-up Argentina, were the surprises of the nine team competition, won by a New Zealand squad that worked with grim determination from that early defeat by Russia to win the final 30-21 before 4,000 spectators at Bayonne.

Few teams were backed by their national unions: even New Zealand players had to pay their own way, subsidised by their clubs, whilst Argentina would only permit one player from each club to be selected to avoid disruption of the domestic season.

The post-tournament dinner started around midnight and ended with a multinational (all except the Russians, who had to catch an early plane) sing-song around the rugby playing guitarists: a spectacle which succeeding tournaments, now under the auspices of the IRFB, are sadly unlikely to repeat.

This quantum leap has been sudden and dramatic: now that in world terms, it ranks second only to the World Cup itself. Indeed, it is only in the past year that many countries have expressed full interest now that geographical play-offs are necessary to reduce finalists to the required 16.

The original nine participants, in order of 1988 ratings, New Zealand, Argentina, France, USSR, England, Wales, Scotland, Italy and Fiji, will be there by right: late 1988 cry-offs Ireland and Romania will be there, whilst the most notable presence is that of South Africa, their first re-entry into the competitive rugby scene. They come face to face with England in their Pool match in Liguria: a confrontation to rouse the rugby world. Japan will also be represented: whilst play-offs between Germany and Holland, Korea and Taiwan and Portugal and Spain will be necessary to decide the final places.

Bedford Modern dominate the line-out, but Bristol Grammar eventually won the *Daily Mail* Under-15 Cup final.

King Edward VI,
Stratford (in blue
and yellow) were
narrow winners of
the *Daily Mail*
Under-18 Cup
final against Bishop
Wordsworth's,
Salisbury.

The ball goes to ground during the Under-21 County Championship final, narrowly won by Warwickshire (in red and white), who beat Hampshire 19-18.

Club rugby in
New Zealand –
University (in
green and black)
versus Linwood in
Christchurch.

Jeremy Guscott
eludes his marker
in the Barbarians'
pool match against
West Germany at
the Hong Kong
Sevens.

The Barbarians, in festive mood during their centenary year, at the Hong Kong Sevens where they lost in the semi-final to Fiji, the eventual winners of the competition.

Emergency
supplies for players
in the Golden
Oldies tournament
in Western
Australia.

The final whistle at the end of the Golden Oldies match between the Puckered Ruckers and The Archives.

Two seasoned front rows prepare to go down in the Golden Oldies confrontation between Jeff Butterfield's Rugby Club of London and Rainbow Coast Tuskers from Albany, Western Australia.

An
uncompromising
approach by the
United States'
winger during the
Women's Rugby
World Cup final
at Cardiff.

According to the recently published Pool details, Australia, USA, Canada, Zimbabwe and Namibia are not represented. Perhaps, even at this late juncture, the position may change but certainly they will be there four years later. No country can afford to ignore a competition with such an international profile.

Organised by CUSI with the collaboration of the Italian RFU under the patronage of the IRFB and FISU, it takes place in Italy from 2–19 July 1992.

Pool A (USSR, Ireland, Italy and Germany or Holland) takes place in Veneto:

Pool B (Argentina, England, South Africa and Korea or Taiwan) in Liguria:

Pool C (France, Scotland, Japan and Portugal or Spain) in Campania, and

Pool D (New Zealand, Wales, Romania and Fiji) in Sicily.

Quarter-finals take place in Sardinia: **Semi-finals** in L'Aquila and Naples: and the **Final** will be played in Ferrara in celebration of the 600th anniversary of that university.

The original age limit of 28, an invitation to the perennial student, has been lowered to 25 (born after 1st January 1967), and players one year out of their studies are permitted to take part to accommodate southern hemisphere countries.

The importance of student rugby in the building of senior national teams is nowhere better recognised than in England and France, perhaps the two countries who gave the first Students World Cup the greatest support from their national unions.

Rupert Moon (above) and Adedayo Adebayo (below), two seasoned club players.

France, who lost 13-11 to England Students in March 1990, after the unsavoury dismissal of two front row forwards, as ever suffer from temperament under fire: but, with the World Cup in mind, their Students team has preference over their 'B' team and boasts potential stars like Philippe Lacroix, who scored ten international tries last season (2 v England, 3 v Wales and 5 v Scotland) at Student level.

England have been preparing for more than a year, starting with their 1990 tour to Namibia and continuing in Canada in July and August 1991 with a squad expected to form the nucleus of the World Cup team under the management of Pat Briggs and coached by Les Cusworth and Jack Rowell.

'B' internationals for England come first so that students such as Hopley, Hunter, Adebayo, Strett, Rodber and de Glanville are unlikely to be in contention, but their very names show the depth of student talent in England which is mirrored in every rugby-playing country of the world.

The England Under 21 squad before their two-match tour to Holland and France.

Wales, for instance, have scrum halves Andrew Booth and Andrew Moore, wing Steve Barclay and Neath centre Jason Ball available, not to mention a host of players in higher education playing first-class rugby and – such is the organizational structure of Welsh rugby – released only reluctantly if at all for college or representative rugby within Britain.

Scotland can call on full international Doddy Weir and Ireland on a clutch of 'B' internationals weaned on league rugby by the presence of their universities in their national leagues.

England beat Wales Students also last year 19-13, and skipper Rupert Moon, the man of the match in the Welsh Cup final for Llanelli, is a common denominator on both England tours and in last season's victorious squad.

England have now elevated Student rugby to separate divisional status, and as such they lost last November to the touring Emerging Australians (what a splendid colonial ring this has!) 22-6. In September 1991 they provide one of the final warm-up matches for England's senior squad before the World Cup with a match at Cambridge, before going on to their own Five Nations Championship.

'B' international Audley Lumsden also toured Canada, recovered from major injury, and team continuity was reflected by the selection for Canada of nine of the Namibian tourists (although Guy Gregory dropped out injured), whilst the emphasis on youth and the future saw the inclusion of five players (Flood, Boyle, Willett, Mallett and Cassidy) from the Students Under 21 team, the first two having also represented England Under 21. The Under 21s are fourth in the national hierarchy and as the majority of the squad have also progressed from 18 Group or Colts the importance of grooming promising players from the earliest age is amply recognised.

Ian Hunter on the attack for England Students against Emerging Wallabies.

But international rugby is only for the elite few students; the importance of the Students League, about to commence its third year in England, cannot be underestimated. Travel costs for the majority of institutes of higher education, with increasingly limited budgets, are restricting participation in this nationwide league which for the majority of students, the future mainstays of club rugby, is the major testing ground.

Neglected for so long by the RFU (details and fixtures of student rugby are not even published in the RFU handbook), there is now the prospect of a limited grant from the Wavell Wakefield Trust for the Students League. But surely the RFU could do more by providing major sponsorship themselves in the absence of commercial support?

Equally importantly, the RFU is working towards the appointment of a Higher Education Development Officer, for which they will provide partial funding, to generate coaching and rugby development for student bodies: but with more than 100 such institutions this might be insufficient. Full funding for the national Student teams on the one hand but limited funding at grass roots level: the story is familiar. Students, with education their priority, cannot be masters of their own destiny in the same way as clubs.

England Schoolboys Under 18 Group line up before their match against the Australians at Twickenham.

Publicity and prestige for national Student teams is good for the game, but the majority of top student players, without such support, would make it to the top through the club route. Whereas grass roots players, as yet without even coaching support, might just resign themselves to opting for one of the other 80 sports competing for their custom (many better presented and organised) if they feel themselves to be the poor relations.

RUGBY WORLDWIDE

AUCKLAND'S ENGLISH COACH
CHRIS THAU talks to MAURICE TRAPP

An Englishman as coach of the All Blacks? "Unlikely, but not impossible," reckons Maurice Trapp, the Englishman extraordinaire, Kiwi by adoption and coach to the normally invincible Auckland side.

Although his coaching credentials are unrivalled he has found out that coaching a side like Auckland can have its unrewarding moments. Maurice Trapp has learned that coaching Auckland is a 'no win' situation. "If the team wins it is considered normal and the stylists criticise the approach, if the team loses the coach is crucified." Trapp, a 6ft 4in giant, born in England 43 years ago, is philosophical about his chance of taking over the coveted All Black job.

"Theoretically it is possible though it is not as simple as it seems. There is very tough competition for the three panel positions. I have already put my name forward as a national selector but I was turned down. Alex (Wyllie) may retire after the World Cup. Alternatively, and I would not be surprised if this is the case, he may decide to stay on to take the All Blacks to South Africa. If he retired his natural successor should be John Hart, but that would definitely finish my chance of being a national selector: two Auckland selectors in the panel is a virtual impossibility."

Maurice Trapp (top) and John Hart (above), the man he succeeded as Auckland coach.

Success does not bring the recognition and respect it deserves in the Land of the Long White Cloud. After his second unbeaten season as Auckland supremo, Trapp nearly lost his position as chief selector and coach to Graham Henry, coach of the Colts side and now in charge of the Auckland 2nd XV.

The first ballot of the Auckland Union Executive was a tie: Trapp and Henry got 13 votes each. Only in the second round did Trapp and his partner and friend, Bryan Williams, manage to get through. This would be regarded as absurd in any meritocracy. However, in New Zealand, where rugby is lived with an intensity unparalleled in any other country, "Success does seem to hurt as much as failure," as Trapp put it. It is the less glamorous side of New Zealand rugby – occasionally petty and often provincial.

Trapp was criticised for what was perceived as a failure to mobilise the full potential of the Auckland side. His critics held him responsible for Auckland's understandable lack of consistency and occasional lapses in commitment –

although they are unbeaten so far, have retained the Ranfurly Shield after a record 42 challenges and won the national championship for the umpteenth time.

"Auckland is a side that coaches itself," said Trapp. "There are 14 world champions in the team and potentially 20 to 25 All Blacks. Each player is an expert, knowledgeable and accomplished. They are driven by a perfectionist streak and my role is to create what I would call the 'environment of success'. It is an environment where players learn from each other, trust each other and motivate each other. I want contributions from each player. I want 15 leaders, 15 decision makers. Each player must feel responsible for the game plan and the way it is translated into practical action.

"The difficulty is to motivate the side. Just imagine how many times these guys have heard team talks about success and the means to achieve it. Think about how many times these guys have won. I don't believe that the role of the coach is to motivate the team. This is the business of the players themselves. This is what makes them play at this level. A coach can inspire a side – yes. A coach can introduce technical innovations. A coach should set goals and advise the means to achieve them. A coach identifies the strengths and weaknesses of the opposition and provides the players with topics for discussion. A coach is a catalyst rather than a motivator. The peer pressure does the rest.

"I have been telling the guys that we must talk more between ourselves about the game, about the opposition, about ourselves. We train Tuesday and Thursday. On Friday we prepare the match. We talk about Saturday's opposition – the backs together, the back row together and then the whole

A family affair for All Black skipper Gary Whetton (above left) at a party to celebrate the 150th Auckland appearance of Grant Fox (above).

The Ranfurly
Shield awaits the
winners of the
match in progress
between Auckland
and Bay of Plenty.

team together. The other day we played against Waikato who had in the front row, Loe, Gatland and Purvis (all All Blacks). That provided our front row guys with a lot of food for thought and discussion."

Trapp's approach to coaching developed from his days as a student at Loughborough University where he played alongside Fran Cotton, John Gray and Keith Fielding in the side coached by Jim Greenwood. Although he had not coached before 1980 when he took over as player/coach of the Auckland side, Ponsonby, his philosophy took shape in the fields of the Midlands and London, playing for Loughborough Students, Harlequins and Middlesex.

"I have learnt more from players, both team-mates and opponents, than I have acquired from any coach. It is your peers who make you who you are. I remember having a virtual training session immediately after a game with Harlequins. This is exactly what is going on in the Auckland team – the players are their first and foremost critics."

In 1974 when he got 'itchy feet', Trapp decided to go on a round-the-world trip. The incentive was an elusive trip to South Africa planned by the Ponsonby club – whom he had played against earlier. Trapp set off overland via Greece, Bulgaria, Turkey, Iran, Pakistan, India, Nepal, Bangladesh and Thailand. He eventually landed in Melbourne where he was working for the underground railway when a call came from Ponsonby – "If you are here by tomorrow at 10 o'clock you can take part in the trial for the South African tour – but no promises".

"After a frantic scramble for a New Zealand visa, I took the first flight to Auckland where I arrived at seven in the morning. I had breakfast with my friend and at 10 o'clock I was playing in the trial. Three days later we were on our way to South Africa. It was a good tour. We lost only two games out of ten. The Auckland press gave the tour, and myself, a lot of publicity."

At the end of 1975, Trapp came back to England and played two games for Quins. He met his wife to be, Gail, and together they looked for jobs as teachers – there were none. He was then offered a teaching position at Henderson High School in Auckland and decided to go to New Zealand. He carried on playing for Ponsonby, coached by Keith Nelson, and then by Lyn Colling and Bryan Williams. He introduced the British maul into the Ponsonby arsenal, preaching that if you have the ball in your hands you can do more things with it than when you have it on the ground.

The Auckland backs – all of them All Blacks – eagerly await possession: left to right, Grant Fox, Craig Innes, Joe Stanley and Terry Wright.

"Ponsonby saw the light," said Trapp. "Lyn carried on coaching until 1980 when I became player/coach with Bryan Williams as my assistant." Under him Ponsonby experienced a remarkable revival. He had a few unbeaten seasons as club coach and in 1984 he became coach of Auckland 'B'. It was a steady progression. After a year off in 1987 he took on the Auckland side.

"Very often an unbeaten record becomes a burden. Look what happened to Canterbury when they lost the Shield in 1985. We are trying to forget about records. We play each game as it comes and try to concentrate on it. We want to win and we are proud of winning. Records are for statisticians. When I coached Ponsonby and we had an unbeaten season, people said that it would never happen again. It happened a few times. Records do not reflect the people who set them."

OK CANADA!

by MIKE LUKE
Manager, Canadian World Cup team 1991

I think we have now started to enjoy the rewards of some good years of preparation going back to long before the first World Cup. That event, in 1987, was a major stepping stone for Canada but it also showed us in stark terms that we still had a considerable way to go. After that there was a major change in coaching style and personnel which has taken us forward into the present era.

Mike Luke in Canadian colours.

Gary Johnson was coach in 1987 and he did a good job before passing over the reins to Ian Birtwell and myself. I suppose that led to a change of approach, based on a more expansive view of the game at international level. Up to the World Cup we had a basic game plan, one set style, and, as the tournament showed, once Ireland and then Wales had worked it out we were sunk. We lacked flexibility.

What we are seeing in the Nineties is a well organised and constructed campaign. We are a conscientious lot, a tight ship in many ways with a Union that does remarkable things with very small resources. I honestly believe we can play a significant role in international rugby in the coming years. I would go so far as to say that the Canadian Rugby Union and, hopefully, the Canadian team, can actually show the way to do things 'right' and show others the way to make best use of their resources.

Canada, as a nation, is a hotch-potch of many different influences, from Europe (notably Britain and France) and Eastern Europe (because of its settlement) but also from the Pacific – Australia, New Zealand, the Pacific Islands, Japan, and most recently, Hong Kong. It's in the Pacific Ring that the majority of Western Canada's business interests lie, rather than in Europe. We are a multi-cultural society and varying influences and styles are reflected in the way we run our rugby affairs. We have a small central office that works extremely well, powered by a lot of very willing competent amateur volunteers. Those people are at the hub of what we have achieved over 18 years, and especially over the last eight, to progress to what is now a respectable position in international rugby.

We have progressed on many fronts. Fifteen years ago the national team played one game a year, ten years ago the one national team made one tour a year. Now there are upwards of 8-10 games a year, an Under 21 team that plays fixtures every year, an Under 19 team that tours in or out every season and has a national provincial championship and an Under 17 national side will take the field during the next twelve months. That has put stepping-stones and targets in place. It has put more coaches into action, more players playing in Canadian colours and a greater generation and publicity of action at both national and provincial level.

At the grass roots level the development of the game has been equally significant. I will take my own province as a case in point. Twenty years ago Newfoundland rugby comprised a collection of students playing the game at university – all expatriates. Now there is a Union with a provincial team that is the fourth strongest in the country, albeit fed by just five clubs. But we now have a junior provincial side and eight rugby-playing schools in St John's, four new rugby fields and a new international standard field which enables us to host important fixtures like the recent one with the New Zealand Development touring squad. Again there are clear landmarks in this progression and expansion of the game.

In terms of playing achievement, Canada's 1991 victory over Scotland was an historic occasion. We had previously tied with Wales, lost to Ireland in extra time, and never quite crossed that hurdle. And as if to dispel any thoughts of a one-off result against Scotland, two weeks later we beat the USA comprehensively – a 30-point win, a significant victory.

These events owe much to the vision of those at the top and here one would have to pay tribute to Barry Giffin, from Alberta, who has done an outstanding job as President during his tenure of office. No longer does Canadian rugby mean British Columbian rugby by another name. People from all provinces feel a part of the Union and when people feel included they will give greater commitment and support – both administrators and players. The Union is now both open and accessible to all.

The public perception of rugby in Canada has been greatly enhanced for two reasons. The World Cup has been crucial. The Canadian Government, that is the Ministry of Fitness and Amateur Sport within Health and Welfare, looked upon rugby for a long time as a British game played by a collection of expatriates for exhibition purposes. There were no world championships, no regional championships, just our annual game with USA. Suddenly a World Cup emerges and we have a measure, a yardstick. We came out of the first World Cup with some credit, and when people judged us 'best of the rest' that was sufficient success to excite government interest. Now we are in the top 16, and maybe we are 9th or 10th and going for better. From nowhere to that, well that's progress. That gives a greater profile for the national team, and more publicity means more interest. That is why winning has been the second major developmental factor, and to capitalise on this we have put in motion a rugby 'caravan' to sell the national team and the game. Players like Gareth Rees have gone into an area a few days before the national team to take coaching clinics, visit the schools, get good television and radio exposure, and press interviews, and generate local interest and pride in a sport in which Canada isn't doing too badly. Three days' preparatory work like that brought 5,000 locals to watch Canada versus Scotland. People then see it, like it and say, "This is good stuff!"

We are by no means complacent, but we do see ourselves as a mid-point between East and West which allows us to blend a bit of what the Aussies do well, on the one hand, like promoting the game to the uninitiated, and on the other hand taking on board some of the great rugby traditions of Europe. We take the best of both worlds and now want to add some character and tradition of our own. We don't any more feel slaves to the European style of doing things, but we are happy to absorb elements that appeal to us, be they French, English or whatever. That applies to the playing side too. I would love to ally some New Zealand forward techniques to some of those enthralling characteristics of French back play! I have a particular love of French rugby that comes from living and playing there myself, and I would dearly wish to impart to Canadian players something of the flair-imbued decision making that would allow our players to be 'spontaneous' in their action within the important code of principles of play that international rugby requires. Personally, I don't believe the French style is 'spontaneous'. I think it is all to do with a perception that comes from their particular approach to the game. They have a greater understanding of the opportunities that the game allows – witness Saint-André's try against England in 1991. That wasn't a fluke creation. It was an understanding, initially by Blanco, then by Sella and Camberabero of the possibilities that were afforded by the distribution of players on the field of play. Wayne Gretzsky has long been Canada's hockey idol – and in my view his greatness owed everything to his perception of the game, above all other qualities of strength, speed and skill. He seemed to have an extra sense that goes beyond the norm – and I believe that is an acquired skill, not an innate one.

Canadian rugby, as I've outlined, moves on apace. We seem to have overcome the hurdles that hampered our early development. Geographical distance affects all aspects of our national life. By living on one seaboard extreme you tend to have to travel furthest, but it doesn't ruffle anybody to get from one side of the country to the other to engage in something 'national'. It is a problem, but it's part of life. Seasonal differences are another factor. In

Mark Wyatt
playing for the
Barbarians at
Cardiff on the
Easter tour.

fact I have played 12-month rugby seasons in the past by moving from east to west according to the time of year. On the East Coast we tend to get under way in late February and play through to September/October, on the West Coast British Columbia play a European season, with a month break from early December to avoid the worst of the winter. Again these regional variations were too often the excuse rather than the problem.

What then of Canada's future? On the international front I suspect that increasingly we shall tend to look towards Australia and New Zealand. We are already involved in the annual provincial tournament with Waikato, Otago, North Auckland – the CANZ event – and, although Argentina are no longer a part because of the cost, we hope that America and Japan will be added to the participants. This could become a major meeting place in between World Cup years.

Cost – and sponsorship – is a major element in all future planning. Our biggest financiers are still the Federal Government, which puts certain constraints on our activities. I suppose it is everyone's ambition to be totally independent. Sponsorship for sport is, however, a fact of life. We are not yet particularly adept at marketing our product though, certainly, the World Cup gives us a great opportunity. If we do well, our task will be that much easier. I would hope that we could achieve something on the lines of what the RFU have achieved with their commercial sponsorship. It's up to us to provide the exciting winning product that will generate that sort of interest. We're making good advances on the television front, but that again puts pressure on us to be successful in the field. Our 24-hour sports channel thinks rugby is fabulous – they revelled in our wins over Japan and Scotland, which they showed live.

I have mentioned earlier about following Australia's path – success on the field, good promotion, good coaching structures generating a wider public interest in the game – these were a characteristic of the Seventies and Eighties. John Howard seemed to be the key man at the helm for Australia. What he has shown us is that, if you want to know how to develop the game in your country, go out to the rugby people and listen to their needs, try to meet them or suggest alternative ways of achieving their goals. His document on this subject is to my mind the blueprint for developing the game in countries such as ours.

We are still small in numbers in global terms. We have a playing strength in Canada of no more than 35,000, of whom about 15,000 are seniors. We can easily double that before the year 2000 if we keep the momentum going. We must build on our growing national sense of identity, build on it so that youngsters feel as I did in the Seventies when as the only non BC player in the national side, I couldn't have cared less if I had had to travel 50,000 miles, not 5,000, in order to pull on the national jersey of the Canadian rugby team. Look at the Maritime provinces now – hosting 14 touring teams this summer (we are the biggest money generator in St John's in terms of sport). Nova Scotia will host the National Championship, New Brunswick hosted the Scottish game. Yes, I am a bit bullish, I think you have to be. The key thing is making sure you have the right people at the helm. Right now we're making good headway.

Naturally we have looked on with interest at the wrangles elsewhere in the world over rugby and the amateur status regulations. It is especially hard to believe this is happening in dear old England. That said, it does not mean that we are lily-white either. This is a factor of success, the more successful, the more difficult it will be to resist those same problems of individuals who will see a chance of making money out of the game. I believe, however, that we have to do what some other Unions have not done, and that is to prepare for that day when players look for financial reward and not wait for it to happen. The New World view says that we want to be pro-active, not reactive, listen to what the players are saying and do our best to respond to those needs, which is not to say that you will meet all those needs. At least one must be prepared to listen and to discuss.

The game is still an amateur game for us. We are not a sophisticated, modern, high-level Rugby Union. We are a relatively small, well-organised and well-run body that manages its affairs well enough.

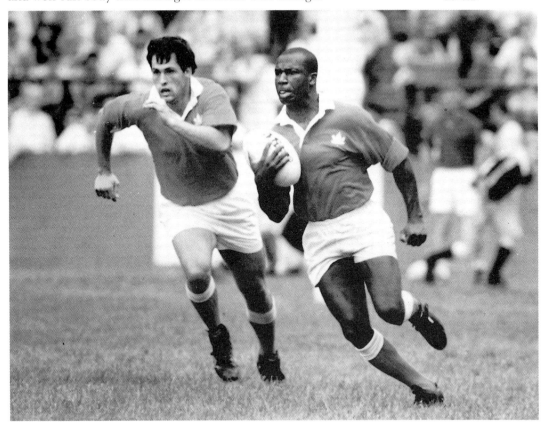

Spencer Robinson sets off on another run for Canada at the Hong Kong Sevens.

THEIR WORLD CUP
by CHRIS THAU

Everything started back in the Seventies when an autocratic dreamer, Albert Ferrasse – until December 1991, President of the French Federation – mentioned the need for a World Championship for the first time.

"It's only natural. It is part of our need for hierarchies," he said at the time. Initially the British derided, then resisted the concept. They rightly felt that a World Cup would fundamentally upset the amateur structure of the game and accordingly affect its ethos.

The southern hemisphere unions, New Zealand and Australia, became, for seemingly different, in fact very similar reasons, the main advocates of a world event. New Zealand wanted a World Cup to counter-balance the perceived loss of popularity of rugby challenged by soccer and basketball in the wake of the disastrous South African tour and shady Cavaliers affair.

The Australians wanted a premier event, similar in glamour and kudos to the Olympics, which would concentrate the minds of their stars, tempted by the huge Rugby League pay deals, to stay in the Union game for at least a four-year cycle.

The combined Antipodean effort, and with the help of the late John Kendall-Carpenter, the England representative on the Board, who actively voted against the wishes of his Union, the 1987 World Cup was born.

The first World Cup was an invitational event, based on the past performances of the 16 participating nations. Naturally, the selection was contentious and disputed at the time by both South Korea and Western Samoa. However, the 1987 World Cup was a success, mostly because it was held in the rugby-mad New Zealand, and not necessarily because it was shared with Australia where the event enjoyed local (in Sydney and Brisbane), rather than national prominence.

The main conclusion of the marketing agents of the 1987 World Cup was that dividing the tournament between two nations is a recipe for disaster. Accordingly, the next World Cup was divided between three countries, Britain, Ireland, and France, with the 'added advantage' of having to duplicate everything in two languages.

Of the eight places up for grabs, only five had been really at stake, because all three contenders from the Americas, USA, Canada and Argentina, had their place secured by IRFB order. The only unanswered question in the

Americas pool was who goes where. In the event, the USA Eagles finished last as predicted and landed in the boiling cauldron of Pool One, while Canada surprised everyone, including themselves, by beating Argentina into second place in the Americas hierarchy.

For the other five places, the IRFB presided over a cumbersome qualifying structure, put forward by the French through their Federation Internationale de Rugby Amateur (FIRA). It involved 14 nations in a series of tournaments and knock-out matches, devised by the FIRA experts. The 1991 World Cup started in April 1989 in Tours in France and not in October 1991 in London.

The enthusiasm of the four nations involved in the Tours qualifying round (Sweden, Denmark, Israel and Switzerland) was indeed contagious. The subsequent tournaments, in Madrid, Harare and Italy (Rovigo, Treviso and Padua), gave the World Cup substance and credibility. It also showed that

small nations want, and enjoy, playing each other at their own level of skill and development. The Swiss, Danes, Swedes and Israelis played like devils. No purist could have taken issue with the technical flaws and tactical errors, such was the spirit that galvanised these small nations into World Cup action. This is the lasting memory of the Tours World Cup.

Poland (in white) take the attack to Spain in front of a good crowd in Madrid.

"We know that none of us has a remote chance of reaching the last 16. But that is immaterial. For us, *this* is the World Cup," said Jean-Jacques Zander, a Swede of French origin and one of the leading organisers of the event. The efforts made by the small, poverty-stricken Unions to attend 'their World Cup' talk volumes about the need for a comprehensive international structure to allow the smaller nations to express their international aspiration without fear of going bust every time they travel abroad. Each Swiss player contributed with about £100 to the team kitty to make the trip possible. The Israelis took unpaid leave while their Union had nearly gone broke in order to pay for the flights to Europe. In Madrid, the Polish Union had to squeeze every penny out of their budget to be able to travel to Spain, while Czechoslovakia's defeat by Portugal in a knock-out qualifying game saved the organisers the embarrassment

The Swedish referee makes his point in the match between West Germany and The Netherlands in Heidelberg.

of having to drop one of the participants from the competition for failing to turn up due to financial shortages. The emergence of Ivory Coast on the international scene, ill-disciplined, talented and full of colour and vitality, was made possible by a loan secured from the French Federation and the generous patronage of a few dedicated French expatriates.

The qualifying rounds in Europe have confirmed that the game is in a good shape, though in different stages of development in the 14 participating nations. Italy and Romania are the rightful qualifiers from a pool that took more than a year to unfold. But Spain has given both of them food for thought and the Dutch, who tackled bravely and resolutely, gave the Italians a fright in the final qualifying tournament in Italy. After the Tours tournament, the knock-out stages brought onto the scene the Dutch, Yugoslavs, Czechs, Germans and Portuguese. The Czechs, fielding a young and inexperienced team, knocked out Yugoslavia. The Yugoslavs, like the Poles in Madrid, seemed unable to convince their top players, playing in the French Championship, to turn up for their country in the World Cup.

The Czechs succumbed to a talented and adventurous Portugal, who in turn were made to suffer by the vigorous Dutch, who had earlier tamed Germany. The Netherlands, undoubtedly the most improved European team of 1990, knocked out Sweden, the winners of the Tours qualifying tournament, and managed to defeat both brave Belgium and gallant Poland to join Spain, Romania and Italy in the last act of the European qualifying drama in Italy.

The Tokyo qualifying tournament, was a replica of the Madrid, Tours and Rovigo/Treviso/Padua mini-World Cups. Flawlessly organised by the Japanese Union, it provided a week-long competition, full of drama, suspense and excitement. The Japanese prevailed over their arch rivals, South Korea, while Tonga, deprived of the services of their injured captain, Siaosi Atiola, succumbed to the more powerful and well drilled Western Samoa.

In Harare, the African qualifying round showed the remarkable resources of African rugby. Zimbabwe managed to scrape through for their second appearance in the World Cup tournament, but they were sternly challenged by Morocco, Tunisia and Ivory Coast. The emergence of the warriors from Ivory Coast, the land of elephants, for their first international outing, was one of the highlights of the tournament. Morocco were indeed impressive, and the potential showed by their national, Abelatif Benazzi, wearing French colours, is a telling reminder of the ability and overall capabilities of Moroccan players.

The enthusiasm of the participating nations vindicates the concept of a World Cup. The quality of the games, the endeavours of the participants and the organisational skill of the Spanish, Italians, French, Czechs and Zimbabweans, have been impressive. The hard fought games in Madrid, Harare,

The formidable Belgian front row in Madrid.

Tokyo, Rovigo and Treviso, Tours, Metz and Heidelberg, gave the World Cup credibility and strengthened the position of the International Rugby Board as the governing body of the game. However, the small nations taking part in the World Cup face financial ruin for their brave attempt to compete in the qualifying rounds. The World Cup BV, the commercial arm of the World Cup, does not seem prepared to help the small Unions foot their bills for transportation and hotels. However, the same World Cup BV is underwriting the bill for transportation and full board for the sixteen participants in the William Webb-Ellis tournament. There is no difference, to my mind, between the young men wearing the red jersey of Tonga, and the young men wearing the green jerseys of Ireland. They are all motivated by the same sense of pride, the same desire to win, the same love for the game. They also played in the same World Cup. The absent friends from Sweden, Poland, Yugoslavia and Ivory Coast, have given the participation of Japan, Romania, Italy, Zimbabwe, in the final stages of the competition, credibility.

The issue has yet to be properly addressed and sooner rather than later the Board will have to decide on a divisional structure for the international game. The fact that neither Zimbabwe nor Japan have any hope of upsetting Scotland and Ireland, or that Italy and the USA can hardly dream of beating the All Blacks or England, is an indictment of the present system.

The expected re-emergence of South Africa on the international scene will complicate the issue further. The African continent will need at least two

World Cup slots if the interest in the competition is to be maintained among the smaller African nations. But who will lose one place: the Americas, or Europe? It is obvious that the current structure of the World Cup is far from perfect. A divisional structure, with four divisions of 12 countries each, based on a promotion-relegation system, will solve the problem, allowing CPMA, the commercial arm of the IRFB and World Cup Ltd., to develop a marketing strategy for the entire game, worldwide. This is what I propose:

World Cup Division One – 'William Webb-Ellis' Trophy
(1995 in South Africa): England, Wales, Scotland, Ireland, France, New Zealand, South Africa, Australia, Fiji, Argentina, Canada, Western Samoa.

World Cup Division Two – 'John Kendall-Carpenter' Trophy
(1996 in Japan): Italy, Romania, the Soviet Union, USA, Spain, Tonga, South Korea, Japan, Zimbabwe, Chile, Morocco, Tunisia.

World Cup Division Three – 'Albert Ferrasse' Trophy
(1997 in Paraguay): Ivory Coast, Uruguay, Paraguay, Belgium, Poland, The Netherlands, Portugal, Czechoslovakia, Mauritania, Sweden, Kenya, Germany

National pride at stake: Tunisia in Harare.

World Cup Division Four – 'Prince Obolensky' Trophy
(1998 in Denmark): Denmark, Switzerland, Andorra, Luxembourg, Bulgaria, Yugoslavia, Brazil, Venezuela, Mexico, Uganda, Israel, Hungary, Georgia.

RETURN OF THE SPRINGBOKS
by JOHN ROBBIE

Perhaps the best book on South African rugby is Paul Dobson's *Rugby in South Africa; A History 1861-1988*. At one point in the author's introduction the question is asked, "What indeed would South Africa have been without rugby football?" One is tempted to answer by reversing the question; "Indeed what would rugby football have been without South Africa?"

The contribution to the game by this troubled land at the southern tip of the world has indeed been enormous. However, rugby has really been getting along without the Springboks for most of the decade and it is perhaps more valuable to look at the current state of the game and also consider what South Africa can offer once the politicians get it right.

Most studies of the sporting scene in South Africa end up in an alphabet soup of confusion. By the time NOCSA, SACOS and SANROC are digested, its time to move on to the SARB and SARU. However, a whole army of triple A athletic bodies are waiting just around the corner - and this is the tip of the iceberg. Each sport is similarly littered with acronyms. It is at this stage one usually decides to give it all up and head for the bar!

Regardless of whether or not International bodies accept various sports back into the fold, most realize that the final decision will be made in South Africa. A number of conditions must be satisfied, including unity of all main bodies claiming to represent the sport, genuine efforts to improve facilities and coaching in underprivileged areas and the eradication of apartheid.

It's this last one that causes the problems as the end of apartheid to one value-system may differ dramatically to another. Does a Government that's committed to reform signal the end of apartheid? Or is it that moment when the first voting slip is actually placed in a free and fair election box that calls for the rolling out of the green carpet with the gold piping adorned with embroidered leaping Springboks? Perhaps if you live in a ghetto in Alexandra township your answer might well differ to that of a Transvaal player living in plush Houghton.

However, as SARB and SARU talks continue, let's assume that agreement is reached, reform accelerates and the Boks are back. (Mind you, as the Zebras from South West Africa are now the Namibian Eagles, it could be premature to even talk of the future South Africans being Springboks - but let's assume.) What then can the rugby world expect?

First and foremost people will marvel at the facilities available to visiting sides. The stopping of tours put great emphasis on domestic competition and building and modernisation programmes continued apace. As host for a future World Cup, South Africa has no equal, even ignoring the magnificent rugby weather. Ellis Park, Loftus, Newlands and King's Park are modern Test venues of the highest standard. Throw in cavernous Free State Stadium and vast Boet Erasmus and you have the big grounds necessary. Every other small town has a rugby stadium with stands and lights, so facilities far exceed what is necessary. It is, however, ironic that a World Cup final could in fact be played at the FNB Soccer Stadium just outside Soweto. If its second tier is completed by 1995 it will hold 125,000 seated spectators. What a prospect.

It is harder to analyse the playing strength. Certainly there is abundant talent and enthusiasm. However, there remains some question about just how this talent will adapt once more to the big time. Namibia's performances would indicate that the transition to the first division will not take South Africa long.

The last time that the Springboks played against the British Lions was in 1980, when they were led by Morne Du Plessis.

Ireland were like a breath of fresh air in last year's Five Nations Championship. Playing without a place-kicker was suicidal - but still the side played well and tested the best in Europe. They travelled out of season to Namibia for an expected series win against rugby's newest nation. The result was a two-nil series defeat and no argument at all. Most South African scribes felt that leaving the Currie Cup would be the beginning of the end for the former South Westers. On the contrary. Visits by Wales and France, followed by a tour, helped to sharpen up the Namibians. They learnt to adapt to the ways of the world without losing their traditional strength and fire and are a better side than the one which contested the wooden spoon in its last Currie Cup season. The inference is that players adapt quickly to the world conditions. However, the Test between Australia and England showed that conditions at the top of the world table are much tougher than those in the nether regions. There is quite a gulf. At the beginning the Boks will struggle against the very best.

"Games are won up front," goes the old cliché. There are many exceptions but to be competitive South Africa certainly needs size and bulk. This she has in abundance. Guy Habble, Uli Schmidt and Jan Lock, as a possible front row, will not be troubled by anyone - at least not after a few games of adjustment. Balie Swart, Andrew Patterson and, perhaps the evergreen Frans Erasmus, would be next in line.

Ironically it is at lock, a traditional area of strength that perhaps the nation is most vulnerable. Adri Geldenhuys is a Frank Oliver clone and just as tough but after veteran Vleis Visagie, stringbeans Adolf Malan and Neil Hugo and perhaps, young Kuifie van der Merwe and Steve Atherton there seems to be a shortage. However, the huge size of players playing at Under 20 level indicates that long-term bulk is assured.

Outstanding back-row players grow on trees in South Africa. Wahl Bartmann is still well short of 30, Gert Small is on the way back and with Jannie Breedt still in commanding form at number 8, no problems here. South Africa like New Zealand could pick three or four back rows of almost equal ability. Piet Pretorius of Northerns is a name to be noted for the future.

Scrum-halves Garth Wright and Robert Du Preez make fascinating studies. Garth is small, quick and imaginative. Robert is large strong and very aggressive. Both have genuine pace, good passes off either wing and both can kick well from the base. A Springbok touring party would be well served by that pair.

Naas Botha still reigns supreme at fly-half. His scoring feats are legendary and his competitiveness is still just as keen as it was a decade ago. He will be around for a couple of years yet - and he'll continue to break opposition hearts. Young pretenders are Joel Stransky, Lance Sherrel and even young Hennie Le

Naas Botha playing at Twickenham for the Overseas Unions in the IRFB Centenary match – next time it may be in Springbok colours.

Roux of Eastern Province. None of them is another Naas but certainly they are talented and show a willingness to run at defences.

With Daniel Gerber injury-prone, Michael Du Plessis is still right up there as a leading centre. In fact, judged on his leadership in the North/South game of 1991 he would contest the captaincy with Botha and Breedt. Pieter Muller, Jeremy Thomson, Jannie Claasens and Bernard Fourie would perhaps fight out the other spot.

Wings are still quick in this country. The memories of Van Vollenhoven, Engelbrecht and

55

more recently Germishuys, Mordt, Du Plessis and Reinach are still treasured. Youngsters will in the future similarly revere Pieter Hendriks, James Small, Deon Oosthuysen, Tony Watson and Jacques Du Plessis. In fact the last name could well follow brothers Willie, Carel and Michael into the national side. Perhaps the interesting thing is that most of the wings are small and fast. There are very few bashers and crashers around at the top these days.

Finally full backs. The great Johan Heunis has retired and probably Andre Joubert and giant Hendrik Truter would be front runners. However, Theo Oosthuysen and perhaps even Gerbrand Grobler could come into discussion.

Many very promising players have been left off his list. With international tours up for grabs standards of fitness, dedication and commitment will rise. Coaches will learn quickly and the players will adapt. Certainly if South Africa gets the World Cup of 1995 she will be ready. Even if it is not a home win, rest assured the competition will, for the very first time, give us the champion side in the world.

An empty Ellis Park awaits the return of international opposition.

THE LIGHTER SIDE

A MANIA FOR MEMORABILIA
by JOHN AHERNE

The bug for collecting got hold of me by chance, on 1 November 1980. I switched on Grandstand just to pass the time for a few hours before the Saturday night 'gig'. The Wales v New Zealand game for the Welsh Centenary was the feature, and I suppose the sense of occasion, with the game, interviews with former great, etc., got to me. I began the quest for an All Black jersey! A phone call here and there to a few local Dublin rugby clubs started my enquiries. The advice I got was to ask any multi-capped Irish players if they could help.

Eventually, after many more calls, Phil Orr and Ollie Campbell gave me a Welsh and French jersey just to start me off. Working at Dublin Airport was also a help, as I would meet the international teams passing through, and gradually I was getting a bit of gear here and there – clubs or provincial jerseys, which came in very useful later as swaps.

Two years after the idea first dawned, luck began to run with me. Wellington were here on a short tour of Ireland and there were four All Blacks in the party. I rang their hotel in Belfast and got Allan Hewson. He had an All Black jersey which he agreed to swap for an Irish one. I went to the hotel in Belfast and Allan introduced me to Murray Mexted and Bernie Fraser. They also had jerseys and I arranged to meet them in Dublin at the weekend with the necessary Irish jerseys. A move which paid handsome dividends later on occurred by accident. They wanted to go shopping in Dublin for Waterford crystal and Irish linen. The leading Dublin shop dealing in these items was in Malahide and Ollie Campbell lived there. I brought the boys out there, they got a very good deal in the shop and we had a few drinks with Ollie in his local.

Reminder of a enjoyable shopping trip.

Hewson and Fraser kept in touch by letter, and in 1983 when New Zealand toured Scotland and England Bernie invited me over to the game at Twickers, and he and Mark Shaw gave me their jerseys, sweaters, ties and tracksuits. Mexted gave me a stand ticket for the game.

I was collecting Ray Gravell before the Ireland v Australia game in 1984 and, while we were in the arrivals hall at Dublin Airport, a little known ex-

England international arrived – a W.B. Beaumont? He discovered that I was taking 'the living legend' to Portmarnock Golf Club to meet the Irish players and asked if there was room in the car for him?

"Come into my parlour said the spider to the fly!" I thought. Over a few drinks, Bill asked if there was any particular jersey I would like for the collection – the Wales/England jersey from the Welsh Centenary game vs Ireland/Scotland would be greatly appreciated. He sent it by post the following month, and it is the centrepiece of my collection, as it is featured twice in Bill's autobiography. He is wearing it shaking hands with the Queen, and in it he scored his only try at international level.

John Aherne with the shirt that Wade Dooley wore against France in 1990, as featured on the cover of *Rugby World.*

I went to Nantes in 1986 for France against the All Blacks, with the intention of getting a blue French jersey. Lady Luck intervened again. Outside the ground I met Gerald Davies, who knew me from Dublin, and he invited me to join him for a walk on the pitch before the game! I remained near the players tunnel area during the game and afterwards in the usual French mayhem, with reporters and cameramen pouring into the French dressing room, I slipped in with my 'bag of tricks' to do some negotiating. I asked Jean Condom if he was interested in any of the gear I had on offer, for a blue French jersey. He had already swapped his, but would I take an All Black's instead – Gary Whetton's – I couldn't believe my luck. On the way back to town on the bus with the New Zealand supporters, they must have taken 40 photographs of the jersey, and rubbed it against their faces – sweat and wintergreen and all!

As the collection grew, I decided to specialise, and try and to build my own team. So the quest began to fill the playing positions with the jerseys of the most famous players around, and by God, the decade of the Eighties must have had the greatest rugby superstars ever.

I was at Twickenham for England v Australia 1988 and I had been promised David Campese's jersey. He scored his 27th international try that day. It had been arranged the day before. I flew into London, Friday afternoon, sat in St Grimm's Hotel lobby for two hours, and eventually met Campo. I explained that Andy Harriman was gaining his first cap for England and would probably want to keep his shirt and I had Marcus Rose's No15 and an IRFB Centenary jersey if he was interested. With Campo was a friend of his, Peter Bills of *The Times*. Peter said he would love to have an England shirt. So Campo agreed to the swap. I gave him the two shirts and shook hands on the deal. I was to meet him at the players entrance after the game. My heart was in my boots all day in anticipation, and when I saw the hundreds of Aussies gathered outside that door I thought my chances were gone, but eventually Campo's head peered through the half-open door and I cut through the mob like a bull in a china shop to collect my prize.

The other superstar jerseys I wanted for the team were those of Serge Blanco and Rory Underwood. Rory had played for the Barbarians v Australia in 1984 and was selected again in 1988 for the Baa Baa's v Australia in Cardiff. Now as all collectors know the Barbarian shirt is one of the most difficult to obtain. My research for this venture showed me that Rory had not played against either the Springboks or All Blacks to date. I met him on the training pitch on the Friday afternoon, and opened my bag. He was interested. "Which one are you giving me?" he wanted to know. Both. We agreed to exchange in the hotel after the game and the rest of the British Isles seemed to be there as well. Brendan Mullin, a good friend, saw me and invited me to his room for tea and sandwiches. He rang Rory and invited him over as well. I was very proud to hear Brendan vouch for me when he said to Rory, "You can rely on this guy, he always gets us genuine gear".

My luckiest encounter was at the Five Nations v Overseas XV for the IRFB celebrations at Twickenham in 1986. The jerseys and tracksuits were supplied by O'Neill's International Sportswear of Dublin. This company was aware of my collection and interest in rugby, and, like my chance encounter with Bill Beaumont, I received a call from O'Neill's asking if I was going over for the game. I was.

It seems they had a late request for six extra tracksuits and jerseys, and would I mind delivering them to Ronnie Dawson at the East India Club? As a reward they gave me two jerseys and a complimentary ticket for the Committee Box. After the game I met Wade Dooley, who was injured and could not play, and discovered that he had not got a Five Nations shirt. I promised to make enquiries at O'Neill's on my return, and they sent him one – 48in chest and all. That was the beginning of a long friendship with Wade, who has made a huge contribution to the collection and influenced some other England players to help. This culminated in Jonathan Webb presenting me with Serge Blanco's jersey in 1989. Without Lady Luck, one gets nowhere.

Each year now I try to forecast who will win the big prizes and try to cover my options at the beginning of the season. In 1990 I fancied England or Scotland. Wade Dooley gave me his England shirt from the game against France, and luckily I asked Des Fitzgerald to get David Sole's in the first game of the Grand Slam in Dublin. So now we all know where two of the Scottish captain's jerseys from the four Grand Slam games went – I got the first one and

John,

You may recall my promise to send you a Hawick sweater to mark your kindness in getting me to the airport in time. Did you think I'd forgotten? No chance! This has been in the house ready for sending for ages but I have been particularly busy.

Please accept it with my thanks for your thoughtfulness. Let's hope we'll meet again soon — perhaps at an Ireland v Scotland World Cup final!! All the best

Bill McLaren

Brian Moore prays for the safe arrival of John Aherne! (See page 62)

Carter Holt Harvey Limited

640 Great South Road, Manukau City, Auckland/Postal Address: Private Bag, Auc...
Telephone (09)278-0999/Telex CARHARV NZ 63473/Facsimile (09)277-9755

9th November, 1988

Mr John Aherne,
21, Offington Court,
Sutton,
DUBLIN 13

Dear John,

Thank you very much for the gift that you sent which ... beautiful and something which will find a special pla... home.

I enjoyed very much meeting you in London and will n... through Ireland without giving you a call.

Kind regards,

WILSON J. WHINERAY

J'ai bien reçu votre courrier, et je me réjouis de savoir que vous êtes en bonne santé pour cette nouvelle année —

J'ai vu M. H. Fourès, il y a peu de temps. Il pense à vous, mais il attend de monter à la Fédération Française de Rugby pour récupérer un maillot tricolore pour vous.

J'espère que la température sera plus clémente lors des premiers matches du tournoi, en attendant, retrons près de notre cheminée, il fait toujours plus chaud.

Bien Amicalement

Philippe Sella.

Some of the many letters received from around the rugby world.

Master Peter Phillips got the last one!

England was my banker for 1991, and again Wade obliged with the jersey against Scotland. But a good collector is never satisfied! Philip Matthews, the Irish flanker, was born in Gloucestershire, and his friendship with Mike Teague is well known. So, when Teague scored a try in the Triple Crown decider, I made tracks for Phil Matthews. They had exchanged, and he would be delighted to donate same to the collection. If there are any budding collectors out there, my advice is give it one hundred per cent – you never know your luck.

Another phenomenon which has grown from my friendship with Wade Dooley is that England have never lost when I have watched them, and Brian Moore, who is obviously very superstitious, developed this into a 'phobia'. At the England v Argentina pre-season game, Brian insisted that I be present for all the Championship games: "Even if I have to pay your fare over myself!" After the Grand Slam game v France, I met him in the Rose Room, and he grabbed my shoulders and said, "Don't forget, New Zealand in October – I am paying for your ticket!" By the time this article appears we will see if 'the luck of the Irish' is true or not.

A wall in John Aherne's private rugby museum.

I love the fun and the challenge of collecting, the making of friendships and, a very important thing to me, the sense of history. I feel very proud and humble when players visit my home to see the display of jerseys, and know that they (the jerseys) will be cherished and cared for like children for posterity. Isn't it a shame to think of the famous jerseys that must be rotting away in attics and storerooms all around the rugby-playing world?

I have to be classified a lunatic to pursue a hobby like this but I wouldn't change it for the world! God Bless *Grandstand* and 1 November 1980.

For the record here is my team from the Eighties (from my jersey collection): Serge Blanco, Rory Underwood, Philippe Sella, Brendan Mullin, David Campese, Jonathan Davies, Robert Jones, David Sole, Philippe Dintrans, Iain Milne, Gary Whetton, Wade Dooley, Mike Teague, Jean-Luc Joinel, Graham Mourie. (And the other teams that I could put out in opposition wouldn't be bad either!)

THE QUOTES QUIZ
Match the Name to the Quote
(Answers on page 68)

1. "The All Blacks didn't have that aura of invincibility today. We've made history and we're over the moon!"

2. "When I first coached Gosforth the club won the John Player Cup in 1976 and I thought that if you could do it for a living it would be the best job in the world."

3. "The honour of representing your country has to be the single most important driving force. The England players will be reminded that the graveyard is full of indispensable men."

4. "The leagues have highlighted the weaknesses in the Welsh game as a whole."

5. "I don't believe in the concept of the Divisional matches, and I certainly don't enjoy playing in them."

6. "We were crying our eyes out but we were very calm."

7. "No-one has the right to say that we were wanting money. That's not true."

8. "We can easily find another 15 players to play Scotland in a month if it proves necessary."

9. "Resign? They'll have to kick me out! I believe the real rugby people of Wales will see the encouraging signs within the team."

10. "Rugby union is a referee's game as much as a player's game. It's how he sees it."

11. "Dean Richards is the best number 8 in the world."

12. "I absolutely hate the 48 hours before a big game. It's the fear of failure I suppose and it gets progressively worse."

13. "France are playing rugby as it was meant to be played."

14. "The problem is far more deep-rooted than any one coach can solve."

15. "If their [the players and officials] fame produces money outside the game we have got to accept that."

16. "You [the Press] were so quickly over the top, some of you should have been in the trenches in the First World War!"

17. "At last the glory is ours. The lads deserve it."

Match one of the following with each quote:
A. Geoff Cooke
B. Richard Hill
C. Mark Egan
D. Mike Pearey
E. An un-named RFU Official
F. Will Carling
G. Daniel Dubroca
H. Rob Andrew
I. Ian McGeechan
J. Mike Mahoney
K. Ron Waldron
L. Simon Hodgkinson
M. Wayne Shelford
N. Dudley Wood
O. John Scott
P. Gerald Davies
Q. Nick Farr-Jones

The Spirit of Crecy

by RICHARD JACKSON
Quirister's School, Winchester

Downed by the Scots of Bannockburn, six centuries away,
The path looked bleak for England's lads, and how they rued the day,
But month by month and year by year they slowly rose again;
Their courage grew, their hopes revived, their confidence regained.
The new King Edward roused his troops, removed the Scottish threat,
He quelled the Welsh and Irish too, his mind on France was set.
In thirteen forty-six arose the chance to prove his worth
Against a mighty French array - no equal upon earth.
The odds, it seemed, were far too great, the French looked mightier still,
But English flags in triumph reigned, at Crécy, on a hill.
And now, Sir William, take your stand, and with your trusty knights.
Destroy those Frenchmen once again with Crécy in your sights.
Your men-at-arms are forged in steel, those titans proved in war
Sir Wade of Preston, huge and tall, his "twin" the giant, Paul.
Sir Jason with his comrade knights, Sir Jeff, Sir Brian there.
To face these men in battle's heat, a Frenchman would not dare.
From Leicester's peaceful Close there comes a very warlike Dean
With two brave knights with saintly names as would befit the scene
Sir Michael comes from Gloucester town, Sir Peter further north,
The French will wish they'd never come to face the English wrath!
To follow up this fearsome eight, the mounted men prepare:
To Bath, Sir Richard's name is famed, he plans attacks with care
While brave Sir Robert, Richmond's son, directs his destrier's charge.
Sir William waits, each sinew tense, the long awaited surge:
Beside him is Sir Jeremy, his speed of wide renown
And arrow-like on wings of gold, Sir Rory soon will run:
Sir Nigel, newly called to war, patrols the English right,
Behind them all, Sir Simon stands, his siege-machine on site.
Its accuracy in the fray has broken many a foe
And now it's set to hurl again, its missiles straight will go.
Now fare you well you English lads, we're with you, to a man!
Go forth to battle!   Set your hearts on victory and GRAND SLAM!

PUCKERED RUCKERS IN PERTH
by CHRIS THAU

It is a strange cult. The worshippers gather in mysterious places, away from the public eye and indulge themselves in bizarre orgies of fun, laughter, friendship and occasionally, of athletic eccentricities, generally described as games of rugby. They have been given the name 'Golden Oldies'. They abide by a number of laws, strictly enforced by giggling officials and largely known as Commandments, a cross-reference to a certain book of learning and faith of perennial value and modernity.

1. I will play the game of rugby for the game's sake.

2. I will not remember the score at the end of the game.

3. If I 'made it' during my playing days I will not use that to embarrass others.

4. If I didn't 'make it' during my playing days I will not try and use Golden Oldies to do so.

5. I will at all times during the games respect the older and more decrepit members on the field.

6. I will follow the Golden Oldies philosophy of fun, irreverence and self-indulgence.

7. I will be an ambassador of Golden Oldies rugby and will spread the gospel.

8. I will never miss the opportunity to make friends and renew acquaintances.

9. I will always remember that I am at far greater risk from whatever I may do to myself or have done to me while socialising than anything which may happen to me on the field.

Members of the fraternity explain that there are only nine commandments because the founding fathers of the movement, now aged and with fading memories have forgotten the tenth.

As one of the more learned members of this increasingly large group of over-age teenagers explained gatherings of worshippers, popularly known as Golden Oldies Festivals, have a very serious academic background.

"We don't gather just to drink, have fun and run around in circles. It is far more than that. We gather in an attempt to explain, analyse and possibly find a cure for a very bizarre syndrome, known as the Golden Oldies Complex," he said. "The symptoms are alarming and the disease tends to develop in men over the age of 40, becoming really dangerous in the over-70s.

The Keystone
Cops.

"Those infected become restless and energetic. In any group of more than two they smile uncontrollably and shake the hand of every person with whom they come into contact. They show various signs of terminal lunacy. They disguise themselves as anything from Keystone cops to the Kaiser's bodyguards, and walk about the centre of cities with no shame. They drink large quantities of beer, lager, wine and any other form of alcohol and devour truck loads of food. Occasionally they run with a rugby ball in their hands but seem unable to decide what to do with it. The epidemic cuts across borders, religious beliefs, races and social backgrounds and is spreading fast."

In an attempt to contain the spread of this virulent strain, carriers of the Golden Oldie virus aged 70 or more are forced to wear golden shorts. This identifies them as 'untouchables', and when they are in possession of the ball during play no-one should approach them.

After Auckland in 1987 and Toronto two years later, it was the turn of Perth, the capital of Western Australia, to host the last meeting of the learned fraternity. Over 5,000 overweight and over-enthusiastic participants from 18 countries gathered for the largest single sport event in the word.

The magnitude of the festival can be compared to the size of the Olympics, but, while the old Olympic ideal 'taking part is more important than winning' is increasingly dwarfed by commercialism and jingoism, no Golden Oldie strives for gold and glory, and national anthems are banned. The Olympic motto, Higher, Faster and Stronger, has been replaced by the three F's of the Golden Oldies Festival: Fun, Friendship and Fraternity.

Officially, all 243 matches played on 33 pitches in Perth ended in as many draws. Smiling was decreed compulsory, and the antics of the middle-aged gentlemen, otherwise regarded as pillars of their communities, can only be described as good-humoured hooliganism. Golden Oldies rugby is genuine proof that rugby players cannot grow old gracefully. They may decay, gain weight, lose speed, hair and teeth but they seem unable to age.

It is reported that the Golden Oldie virus was first 'isolated' in Japan right after the war. In 1947, seven former Japanese internationals (I have to be honest and say that I am not aware of any Japanese international encounter before the outbreak of war – but my ignorance has no limits) decided to form a club for players over the age of forty. The club was baptised FUWAKU, which is the Confucianist term 'forty is the age free of vacillation'.

In 1975, one Jeff Butterfield, England and British Lions centre, a Northampton buff and restaurateur, decided to launch a regular event for non-pensionable rugby players. He embarked with a bunch of them on a tour of the West Indies, to be among the first to use the name Golden Oldies. In 1977 he took another group of rugbyholics on a trip to Miami to play other emotionally unstable travellers from other lands. Two years later, a visionary Kiwi, Tom Johnson, convinced Waitemata Old Boys, Bryan Craies – the current chairman of the movement – and Barry Herring, that the idea of gathering the ageing rugby population in one place, at one particular time was worth giving a try. By their own admission, the two were conned into helping Johnson to launch the festival – a modest disaster involving 15 teams and about 400 participants. It was a far cry from the 5,000 strong blast of fun, good spirits and coarse rugby that hit Perth at the end of May 1991.

Cyril Andrews, a 1937 Wallaby, leads the parade of the Queensland XXXXs from Brisbane.

Former Scotland international and British Lion, Bill Cutherbertson, at the helm of a multinational selection known as Puckered Ruckers was delighted with the atmosphere of the Festival. "I did not know about these festivals before. I played in Bermuda with the Scottish veterans, but that was almost serious international rugby. This is such great fun. The idea is brilliant and deserves more popularity. We played 12 games in 12 days and used a different type of warm up and a different language every time we played."

Alongside the humorous Scot was the famous Irish *agent provocateur*, giggler and impersonator, Micky Quinn, who agreed to star in the Puckers' feeble exercise in cowardice, scheming and alcoholic torpor against an equally decrepit local side, known as Messenger's Marauders. Quinn, whose self-deprecating humour was greatly enjoyed by everyone, was in Perth as part of Lansdowne's impressive presentation of the Dublin 1993 festival. Perth beat nine other contenders for the 1991 Festival. The ailing economy of the Western Australian

Bill Cuthbertson (second from the left) in pre-match ritual with fellow Puckered Ruckers.

capital was boosted by an injection of about 18 million Australian dollars. The next festival will inject about 20 million punts into the economy of Dublin, while the profits of the event will go towards developing youth rugby in Ireland. As Quinn put it, "We don't ask you to come to Dublin. We don't invite you to come to Dublin. We demand we see you in Dublin in two years time!"

Answers to The Quotes Quiz
(see page 63)

1 – Q; 2 – J; 3 – A; 4 – O; 5 – B; 6 – C; 7 – F; 8 – E; 9 – K; 10 – I; 11 – M; 12 – L; 13 – G; 14 – P; 15 – D; 16 – N; 17 – H.

LOOKING BACK

IT'S NOT THE GAME WE KNEW
by HARRY TOWNSEND

Rugby must have been real fun in the old days! Laws were few and people did things themselves just to get the game going. Present day rugby officials would have heart attacks at some of the early goings-on: but as time passed fun was legislated out until today even nostalgia isn't what it used to be.

Richard Mullock, Newport secretary in 1880, was convinced that at a meeting in the Tenby Hotel, Swansea, he had been elected to arrange the first England v Wales match and to pick the Welsh team. Everything went wrong; but he still struggled on. The trial match was cancelled, the match date was re-arranged twice, the day of the actual match clashed with a Welsh semi-final cup tie: and when the team arrived at Richardson's Field, Blackheath, they were two men short.

Two Welsh students in the crowd were co-opted and the team shuffled to accommodate them. Ten minutes into the game, two players were injured and had to go off: and of the thirteen remaining, Godfrey Darbishire hadn't played for two years.

Under the circumstances they did well to lose by a drop goal and thirteen tries, seven converted: 69-0 in today's scoring. But at least Mullock had got Wales on the field, and in scarlet jerseys with the Prince of Wales feathers and the motto 'Ich dien', instead of the black jerseys with a leek favoured by the rival South Wales Football Union. A year later Wales beat Ireland in Dublin: they were on the march.

Wales started in the colours that they were to keep, which is more than New Zealand did. They toured New South Wales in 1884 wearing dark blue shirts with a gold fern leaf: they changed to black shirts and white shorts in 1894, and finally moved to all black in 1901. But they didn't get their nickname of the All Blacks until 1905: the result of a Welsh printer's error in giving the New Zealand team colours in the programme as 'All Blacks' rather than 'All black'.

South Africa registered their first international victory in 1896 wearing green shirts, beating the British Isles 5-0. The captain, Basil Heatlie of Diocesan Old Boys, had brought along his club shirts as South Africa had none of their own and, although his club had disbanded by 1903, the outfitters still had some green shirts with white collars in stock to which were added black shorts and the red socks of the Villagers Club in Cape Town: colours which were retained until 1937 when collars became old gold, shorts white and socks green.

Although rugby had been played pre-war in Czechoslovakia, founded it is said by Andrej Sokora (a writer of children's books), the game boomed in Prague during the war when the Germans forbade large gatherings in the city unless it was for sport. As they generally didn't know anything about rugby, it was allowed to continue. Each club became a cell of the Resistance, and went into action when the Allies rolled into Czechoslovakia.

Sadly Czechoslovakia now languishes in Group B2 of the FIRA championship, one grade above Andorra, whilst Switzerland currently do not participate although they reached unheard of rugby heights when they pressed the coach driver into action on tour. He did so well that they kept him in the squad.

Western Samoa, now renowned for their spectacular running rugby, did not play their first international until 1924 when they entertained Fiji. As the team had to go to work, the match began at 7 o'clock in the morning. Fiji won 6-0 despite having to avoid a large tree in the centre of the pitch.

One of the most obstinate teams must be that of the small town of Vergt in the Dordogne. Playing in the French Third Division in 1984, four players were suspended after a particularly rough match, and they made their unique protest against what they considered an unjustly harsh sentence by playing their next league fixture with only eleven players against Lermont. They stood like statues as Lermont ran in the tries: the referee abandoned the match after ten minutes with Vergt losing 42-0. The next week the referee let the

Re-enactment of the birth of the game at Rugby School.

match run it's full length and Gujax Mestras won 236-0, and the third week they really surpassed themselves against Lavardac losing 350-0, surely the highest score on record?

Touring teams always have the advantage of togetherness, but no touring team has equalled the record of the British Isles in South Africa in 1891. They won all 19 matches, scoring 224 points to 1: a try by Versfeld in the first match.

For different reasons, few teams can approach the extraordinary tour of the first British Isles team to tour Australia and New Zealand in 1888. After 9 matches in New Zealand, they went to Australia to play 35 matches. 19 turned out to be Aussie Rules, their captain, R.I. Seddon, was drowned in a boating accident, and they then returned to New Zealand for a further 10 matches.

Tours in those days were long drawn out, with only sea travel. None more so than the New Zealand Native team of 1888-9 which lasted about 21 months and included 104 matches in New Zealand, Australia and Britain, with Davy Gage playing 68 of 74 matches in Britain. How did they fare? They won 78, lost 20 and drew 6 and were glad to get home.

It's strange to think of the success of the World Cup: strange, because this could have happened years before when rugby was an Olympic sport. It was a major sport at the Paris Olympiad of 1900. Baron Pierre de Coubertin, founder of the modern Olympics, was a rugby player and refereed the first French cup final. Only three teams took part: France, Germany (represented by PSV Frankfurt) and Britain (Moseley Wanderers). France beat England 27-7 and Germany 27-17: and, as Germany did not play England, Germany won the silver medal for losing by the least margin.

London in 1908 attracted only two entries: England (represented by champion county Cornwall) and Australia, currently on tour. Australia won 32-3. It is a matter of conjecture who won in Antwerp in 1920. USA, represented by Stanford University who had expected to play American Football, claim to have beaten France 8-0. France claim victory 14-5. Historians generally accept the American version.

The last time that rugby was played at the Olympics was in Paris in 1924. The American enthusiasts, again largely from Stanford, easily beat Romania as did France. Then, to the surprise of a highly partisan crowd, USA beat France 17-3 including five tries, to retain the gold medal. USA are therefore still undefeated Olympic rugby champions.

It's an extraordinary story, as is so much of the early history of the game. Now you see why I say that much of the fun has gone out of the game. It's not the game that William Webb Ellis (did he ever run with the ball?) knew. But that's another story.

25 YEARS AGO

From the pages of *Rugby World*

January 1967

January bears an unfamiliar look in the year of 1967. For as long as I can remember the England v Wales match has taken place on the third Saturday of the month but this time it has been moved forward to April 15, when far better playing conditions can be expected. No-one will complain about that – remembering the January mud-baths of recent years – but it is a pity that the new date for the fixture in Cardiff clashes with Ireland v France in Dublin on the same day.

.... Rugby has all too few really big occasions and there is a great deal to be lost, publicity-wise, by cramming the whole international match programme into fewer Saturdays.
Vivian Jenkins, Editorial

The fact that you play friendlies is reflected in your national team. You can hardly complain about lack of success in international matches if, throughout the structure of your game, there is little incentive to win.
Tommy Bedford, Oxford University and South Africa

Fly to Dublin or Paris for an international match weekend – for the Dublin match all in cost 17 guineas, for the Paris match 14 guineas, from London, including return flights, two nights, good class hotel with B and B, plus match transfers and courier.
Rugby World advertisement

H. Steele, No 8 from Rainey Endowed School, Derry, on tour in Surrey showed that he should soon make a name for himself in first-class rugby.
George Abbott, Schools Round-Up

Colin Payne of Harlequins, asked about the condition of Quins' full-back, Tudor Williams, who was concussed during the match with London Welsh, said: "I knew he was OK. When I asked him what day it was, he replied 'Yes'".
Pat Marshall

A recent survey of 60 players in South Wales revealed that over a third of them had broken their teeth while playing rugby, a situation which would not have arisen had they worn properly fitting mouthguards.
A dental surgeon

Left Tommy Bedford in action for the Springboks.

February 1967

Many people for a long time have been advocating that neutral referees should be exported and imported for international matches on major tours, but the authorities, so far, have fought shy of this. I think they are wrong – having seen the refereeing troubles caused by refereeing on five Lions tours – but there is no sign at the moment, of any move to put things right.
Vivian Jenkins, Editorial

It is a fact that Wales do better when they have a large number of long-serving players in their ranks.
J.B.G. Thomas

Gordon Bendon. This tough 'warrior' seems to have taken a new lease of rugby life... now 37 and in his nineteenth season with the Wasps 1st XV.
Roundabout

The Welsh Secondary Schools XV win possession against England.

Welshman Gwynne Walters created a new record when he refereed the Varsity Match in December, the seventh time he had handled the game, one more than Cyril Gadney and the late Albert Freethy.
Roundabout

Kevin Andrews at the head of a Staffordshire team of virtual unknowns from clubs like Stoke-on-Trent, Madeley College, Walsall and Old Dixonians, sent supporters wild with delight with his county's success over Warwickshire.
Roundabout

Two Italian players, Guedo Fattori and Roberto Lenzi, caused quite a stir at North Durham club for both turned out to be international players.
Roundabout

Between 1946 and 1966, England had 19 captains – eight outsides and eleven forwards...One can build strong theoretical cases for certain positions, but, basically, it is the man who matters.
Michael Williams

Australia shock Wales 14-11, but what a memorable game!
Picture report on December's international, when Alun Pask was Wales' captain

I.R. Shackleton has played well in a fast-moving set of backs for Bradford GS...Neath GS's two outstanding players, I. Wagstaffe and J. Bevan, have both been picked for the Welsh Secondary Schools XV.
With the Schools

Ian Smith (Edinburgh University) has, as they say, a comfortable figure, but he also possesses a developing sense of position, good hands and an especially potent left foot.
Norman Mair

Did you know that Joe Erskine, of boxing renown, was a very good rugby player as a lad, playing junior international rugby for Wales in 1950 at fly-half?
Sides and Asides

Springbok captain and scrum-half, Dawie de Villiers, has been ordained as a clergyman in the Dutch Reformed Church of Stellenbosch.
Reg Sweet

March 1967
The International Board keeps things very much to itself and Joe Bloggs of the Extra 'B' XV has to take what is coming to him and lump it.
Vivian Jenkins, Editorial

I heard Tom Berry, until recently chairman of England selectors, saying after Australia's 23-11 win over England at Twickenham, "I really begin to wonder whether we shouldn't bring the Australian kicking-to-touch law into general use." He had obviously been impressed by the Wallabies' handling and running, and small wonder.
Vivian Jenkins

A more constructive approach and determined attitude would, I feel, improve the modern concept of the game more than the manipulation and changing of the laws.
Cardiff and Wales new 22 year-old centre, Gerald Davies

Rugby is such a bloody silly punishing game that the only justification for playing it is success.
J H R 'Dick' Greenwood

The question of out-of-pocket expenses for touring rugby players has developed into one of the major off-season discussion points in New Zealand. The general feeling seems to be that 10 shillings a day is not enough, especially when touring the British Isles.
Donald Cameron

April 1967
Brigadier H L Glyn Hughes, President of the Barbarians, spoke for a lot of people when he said at the dinner following the Baa-Baas v Australians match in Cardiff: "Can't we possibly simplify the laws?"

If (our national) teams want to beat the All Blacks next season, it will not be enough just to foregather for 48 hours before the match and hope for the best.
Vivian Jenkins, Editorial

Ray Williams, the newly-appointed coach/organiser to the WRU, hopes to take up his duties on June 1st.

There is no need to go into that dreary business about England's two victories in 17 games...the truth is that success and failure go in cycles.
Rupert Cherry

The thing was to get a side who would all play the same style, although they might not be doing it for their own clubs or counties.
M.R. Steele-Bodger, Chairman of England Selectors

I am sick and tired of people saying that we must have open football. Let's get the game won and realise that, if you can't win up front, then you won't win at all.
Eric Evans, England Selector

May 1967
Ludlow GS, won 22 of 23 matches, and an interesting feature was that the XV contains 4 brothers, the Griffiths.
With the Schools

Noel Murphy (Barbarians) and John Thornett (Australia) lead out their teams at Cardiff.

Ian McCrae of Scotland is tackled by England's Bob Taylor in the 1967 Calcutta Cup match.

There were tears in the selectors' eyes, I am told, when England brought off their sensational grandstand finish in the Calcutta Cup, scoring 11 points in 6 minutes.
Vivian Jenkins, Editorial

'Loiterers' will no longer be allowed to enter the maul from the 'wrong side' when they are returning from up-field.
Changes to the Laws

Out-half, Michael Gibson, is certain to be the biggest attraction.
Ireland Tour of Australia, preview

Peter Ford, now 34, recently played his 500th game for Gloucester.

Coventry and England international, Rodney Webb, and his brother Richard, a Wallaby, are two players who have advanced to senior status via Newbold-on-Avon RFC.

Last Christmas Eve, three days after leaving Monmouth School, centre Keith Jarrett, made his debut for Newport at Ebbw Vale. Overnight he became a star.
John Billot [Later that season Jarrett scored 19 points for Wales v England]

June 1967

"It was a circus turn and we apologise for it," wrote a correspondent of *L'Equipe* about the parade, with banners and placards, of a hundred or so of his compatriots before the kick off of this season's England v France match at Twickenham. "Ridiculous chauvinism," he commented.
[France won, 16-12]

Cliff Jones, chairman of the Welsh selectors, has suggested that Unions should be allowed to bring their players together at any time within the 14 days after the teams for an international match are announced.
Comment

There are about 500 players in Holland, and fourteen clubs.
[There are now 106 clubs and about 9,000 players]

Mr Freddie Baynes, a Vice-President of the Shelford club, runs the line each Saturday for the 1st XV. Mr Baynes is 80!
Sides and Asides

Full marks to the Welsh Boys [Wales Schools beat England 8-5] for excellent tackling and covering – especially J Williams [J P R] of Millfield for a great exhibition at full-back.
With the Schools

Thanks to Jarrett, Wales avoided a 'whitewash' and the 'Big Five' – Rees Stephens, Glyn Morgan, Cliff Jones (Chairman), Harry Rowcott and Alun Thomas, breathed more freely.
J.B.G. Thomas

July 1967

As for world records, what about Guy Camberabero's 27 points for France against Italy?
['Son of Guy' – Didier Camberabero scored a world record 30 points for France in their 1987 World Cup match v Zimbabwe]

Ireland's win over Australia in Sydney was a timely blow for the rugby prestige of the Home Countries. The financial success of the tour may also mean that Australia, in future, will be able to mount their own tours, instead of being tagged on to those to New Zealand.
Vivian Jenkins

Prop Phil O'Callaghan, reserve scrum-half Liam Hall, Sam Hutton and Ken Goodall, emerged as Ireland's leading characters.
Peter McMullen

The Scottish Borderers attracted 70,000 to their 4 matches on tour in South Africa, and their highlights were the 23-all draw with Transvaal and the 15-8 defeat by Natal. In Jim Telfer they had a splendid leader and a tremendous worker on the training field.
Reg Sweet

August 1967
It was a tough start getting the Welsh rugby crowd on your side. In the Cardiff v South Africans match in 1951, whenever I started the band on a tune the crowd would wait, then start up a different one. This happened three times.
John Williams, conductor of the St Albans Military Band which lead the singing at Cardiff Arms Park

Cornish Rugby is Not to be Mocked.
Heading to article by Alan Gibson

There was much eating and drinking, much singing and dancing, much reminiscing and back-slapping – but few chaps got off-side. Harlequins you know.
Anonymous report on Harlequins Centenary Ball at Twickenham

With the body fit for rugby we can cut down injuries by 50 per cent.
Danie Craven, in an article describing the 30 pieces of training equipment on his campus at Stellenbosch University, an array ranging from old car tyres suspended in mid-air for diving through to an 80lb river stone used for weight training

Few women can be more knowledgeable about the game than Mrs Mainwaring, a cheerful supporter, who does not hesitate to say from the grandstand what she thinks about the game.
Profile of Mrs Mainwaring's son, Haydn, Aberavon and Wales lock

September 1967
At training, when neither hustled nor pressed, I can reach up to 27 yards – in matches, around 22 yards.
Lilian Camberabero (height 5ft 4in, weight 10 stone), describing his scrum-half pass

Abertillery salutes two great internationals retiring at the same time – Haydn Morgan (27 caps), Alun Pask (26 caps).

Selection is a matter of opinion anyway. If they pick you, you're the lucky one.
Bob Hiller

Left Billy Hunter of the Scottish Borderers claims a line-out ball with support from Norman Suddon, in the match against Natal.

Springbok rugby once knew a period of just on 60 years when not an international match series was lost. It has since sampled its full quota of years in the wilderness.
Reg Sweet

Memorable Springbok Revival.
Headline to report on South Africa's 26-3 win over France

The greatest game I've ever seen.
Wilf Wooller, on Wales v England, 1967

As for toilet-roll throwing, I think we have stopped that by making the people who throw them see how ridiculous they are.
Robin Prescott, RFU Secretary

The RFU's surplus for the 1966-67 season after taxation was £40,319. During the past year membership totalled 1,625 clubs and 869 schools, whilst 111 clubs applied to tour and 51 clubs entertained overseas visitors.

A newspaper broke the story that 11 former All Blacks would not be invited to the NZRU 75th jubilee celebrations because they had switched to rugby league.
[Not so in 1992 – Centenary of NZRU]

October 1967
Canada's Centennial will be marked by the match in Vancouver when Canada play England in the first full international staged in Western Canada. Canada have only once previously fielded a national side – in September 1966, when they lost 8-19 to the British Lions in Toronto.
Bob Spray, President of the Canadian Rugby Union

Gradually the WRU's message about coaching is getting through. Most clubs have appointed men to take charge of training sessions, advise captains and sit in when teams are chosen.
Ron Griffiths

The vacant Cardiff fly-half spot is now being occupied by Barry John, capped twice last season, who has left Llanelli, where Phil Bennett, the Wales Youth skipper, is the favourite to succeed him.

We shall want our forwards to get the ball out. They cannot do that if they are having a punch-up. If we encounter dirty play we shall have to grin and bear it. I certainly would not advise our chaps to retaliate.
David Brooks announced as Lions Tour manager for 1968 to South Africa, responding to a question on dealing with foul play

After Wembley, unlike the rugby union internationals, there was no social get-together between the opposing sides, each team organising its own entertainment. This is typical of all league games, where there is very little social contact between teams. But this is to be expected in a professional game, where the criteria is to make money rather than friends.
Tom Brophy reflecting on his early experiences having switched codes to rugby league

November 1967
Another All Blacks tour is upon us and everyone will hope this time, that it will be remembered for its rugby, not for the rows and 'incidents' that have besmirched so many major tours in recent years.
Vivian Jenkins, Editorial

Brian Lochore – Farmer
Ian Kirkpatrick – Farmer
Ken Gray – Farmer
John Major – Farmer
Colin Meads – Farmer
Sid Going – Farmer
Murray Wills – Farmer
Alan Smith – Farmer
Sam Strahan – Farmer
Jack Hazlett – Farmer
Kelvin Tremain – Stock Agent
From Pen Portraits of Players *in the magazine*

The 1967 New Zealand party should develop into a strong party.
Preview Comment [NZ Tour Record in Britain, P 15 W 14 D 1]

In my view play is dull and drab now teams have the idea that they must not lose, so they do not take the risk of passing the ball.
Barry Cumberlege, England 1920-23

Reserve front row for the All Blacks: (left to right) Ken Gray, John Major and Alister Hopkinson.

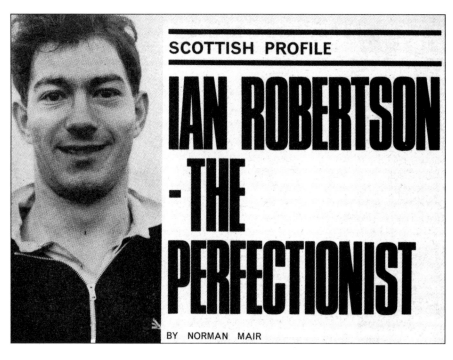

SCOTTISH PROFILE

IAN ROBERTSON - THE PERFECTIONIST

BY NORMAN MAIR

December 1967

Q: Why has this page got a black border?

A: Because it's a lament for rugby players.

Q: Why mourn them?

A: Because they seem incapable of supporting a magazine devoted entirely to their great game.

Appeal for new subscribers to Rugby World

First there came the various teach-ins before the England team set off on its short tour of Canada, and also the three trial matches against the Midlands, South of England and North of England, then there was the tour itself, and now a respite. Oh no! In the next month or so England will be holding three more trial matches, one in Falmouth, one in Durham and one at Twickenham, one every two weeks. All this to produce a selection to meet Wales in January. Small wonder if the clubs should complain!

Vivian Jenkins, Editorial

Ian Robertson – The Perfectionist.

A neatly proportioned 5ft 9in, weighing just under 12 stone when fully fit [was he ever?], Robertson has powerful hindquarters [That's where he got his interest in horse racing from!] ...Robertson on his day [I must have missed it! Ed] can handle as dexterously as most. He knows how to tackle [Ah! But did he put his knowledge to the test?] ...Robertson likes to run the ball, "often, I suppose, when I really shouldn't." [How true!] ...A perfectionist, apt to allow a bad start to affect his whole match [Now we know the problem, I'd often wondered.] ...at 22 [was he really that young once?], he still has time to acquire the necessary resilience [Yes, and we're still waiting.]

Extracts from the generous pen of Norman Mair, with additional editorial comments from the subject's co-editor

ENGLAND AND WALES IN AUSTRALIA

A BACKWARD STEP FOR ENGLAND
by IAN ROBERTSON, BBC Rugby Correspondent

In March, England were sitting on top of Everest after beating France at Twickenham to collect their first Grand Slam since 1980. They were the undisputed champions of Europe and the northern hemisphere and were installed as second favourites for the 1991 World Cup behind the defending champions, New Zealand. The four-week tour of Australia in July changed all that.

It was always going to be difficult to parachute into the middle of the Australian domestic season from the middle of the English close season and do themselves justice, and so it proved.

For the opening match the New South Wales side took the field after an unbeaten run of eight matches in ten weeks, including a short tour to Argentina. None of the England team had played a single game of rugby in the previous two months. It was hardly surprising that the Australian players were much sharper, more match-hardened and fitter and they beat England by 21 points to 19.

It was no disgrace to lose by two points to New South Wales especially when Wales lost 71-8 the following week, but it was a set-back and it was bound to affect both confidence and morale. The following week a loss to Queensland by 20-14 was a further blow but it was still not disastrous as the only matches which really mattered on the tour were the two Tests.

The first against Fiji in Suva was won in rather dramatic fashion. On a hot, humid afternoon, the English forwards played good controlled rugby in the first half to take command of the game just as they had done so many times in the previous three years in the Five Nations Championship. Unfortunately, they did not take every scoring opportunity but still built up a comfortable lead after half an hour of 12 points to 3. Webb converted a try by Probyn and kicked a penalty while Andrew dropped a goal.

However, Serevi, who had kicked an early penalty for Fiji, converted a try by Seru immediately before half-time and he dropped a goal straight after half-time to level the scores at 12-12. For the next 20 minuted Fiji were camped in the England half and came close to scoring on many occasions. It was a great tribute to the English defensive organisation and their tremendously competitive nature that they prevented Fiji from scoring and it was even more remarkable in the oppressive conditions that they were able to summon up the

energy to launch a furious counter-attack in the last quarter of an hour to rattle up 16 points and clinch a notable victory.

Rob Andrew ripped the Fijian defence apart with a spectacular break in midfield which ended with Rory Underwood scoring his 28th try. Andrew, enjoying a purple passage of play, dropped his second goal of the match and then scored his first try in international rugby. This was a well-deserved, hard fought victory.

A win in the last Test against Australia would have clinched a wonderful six months for England but it was not to be. In a magnificent game of rugby at the Sydney Football Stadium the Wallabies produced a breathtaking display to beat England quite handsomely by 40 points to 15.

This included a try count of 5 to 1 in Australia's favour. Roebuck scored one and Campese and Ofahengaue got two each. That incredible points-scoring machine Michael Lynagh added four conversions and four penalties to top 600 points in international rugby.

It was not that England played particularly badly so much as Australia played stunningly well. Webb converted a try by Guscott and kicked three penalties. But even though England boldly and bravely tried to play running rugby they were just unable to create enough scoring chances and when they did have the odd opportunity the Australians tackling and covering was outstanding.

The score probably flattered Australia but the crucial fact was that the English pack was outplayed for the first time in a long time. The forwards scrummaged well but the Wallabies held the initiative at the line-out and were a yard faster in the open. One or two of the ageing English forwards began

Martin Bayfield had a torrid time against John Eales in the Test against Australia, although (above) he did win the duel on some occasions.

to look their age. There is little doubt that this England side peaked gloriously in the Five Nations Championship and they may never quite recapture that form again.

By the time of the 1992 tournament, there will be, almost inevitably, a few changes in personnel. The heroics of the Grand Slam are written in bold capitals in the history books and can never be taken away. Nonetheless, in Australia, the team took several steps backwards and they were no longer quite the force they had been.

A let-off for England – John Eales breaks through the English line, but the ball was to slip from his grasp before he could touch down.

It seemed that they had tried to cross one bridge too many and had paid the price. The England team manager Geoff Cooke, who, along with Roger Uttley had masterminded the Grand Slam, sensibly said at the outset of the tour that he wanted to find out if the champions of the northern hemisphere were as good as the best in the southern hemisphere. He found out. Sadly, they were not.

WALES – EVER DOWNWARDS
by LYN DAVIES

For those with powers to interpret these things the omens were there right from the outset. No flight ticket booked for the travelling immediate past President, the unearthly arrival time at a locked-up, blacked-out, damp hotel and the storms and electrical failures of the next eight days should have been ample warning of the disasters that were to follow.

In hindsight, of course, it all seems so plain. One can even go back further and ask whether this was the right tour to undertake, bearing in mind Wales's recent record and the fact that Australia were to be in the same World Cup group. Planning and organization, however, had never been the Welsh Rugby Union's forte and on this tour, as never before, its shortcomings were to be exposed.

Time-wise few touring parties have had a better period of preparation. For six weeks before departure twice weekly training sessions had been held. Time, that in theory should have been used for welding the squad into units; time that in practice was far too often spent on long distance running. Meritorious though high fitness levels are the advantages are for the most part negated unless players know the where and when of events.

In organisational terms, therefore, the party was always in the catch-up phase. Even that eight-day period in Perth with just the one game against Western Australia was spent on overlong fitness sessions. No wonder, therefore, that the game situation caught so many people by surprise. Overshadowed as it was by a local Australian Rules match, the game against West Australia was a low key

An all too familiar position for the Welsh on their Australian tour, as they stand on their own goal-line watching another conversion attempt.

affair. What was made glaringly obvious though was that the party would encounter great difficulty in gaining both line-out and second-phase possession. With pushing and lifting the order of the day at the line-out and diving on the loose ball the norm at the breakdown, it was a warning that for the rest of the tour Wales would be starved of possession.

However attractive the thought of Brisbane and the Gold Coast with its warmer climate, welcoming accommodation and sophisticated facilities, there wasn't a great deal of confidence as the tour moved eastward from its none too strenuous opening to Australian rugby reality. Queensland weren't at their strongest having twice lost to arch rivals New South Wales, but without doubt this was to be the touring party's first real test.

Unprepared for such an onslaught of pace and purpose, Wales within the opening quarter were 20 points adrift. Seemingly even more shocked were the Queenslanders; Lynagh missed with numerous kicks at goal, final passes were either dropped or not given, and what should have been an opening half romp developed into nothing more than a comfortable lead – a lead that became increasingly uncomfortable. At one stage Wales came back to within two

The Welsh squad at their pre-tour training camp.

points at 22-20. However, that shock seemed to jolt the Queensland team out of its stupor. Lynagh rediscovered his kicking boots and a comfortable victory was achieved, although the final scoreline of 35-24 did nothing to reflect the huge gulf that existed between the two teams. Nevertheless that margin fooled the Welsh party into believing that the outcome was achieved by its own powers of recovery, when the reality was that so undemanding had the Queenslanders found the opening quarter that concentration had been completely lost. It was slackness on their part rather than Welsh efforts that had made it a contest.

Encouraged by that performance and not tested in the swamps of Canberra there seemed more optimism than was warranted as the touring party made its way for the fateful encounter at Sydney. With nine straight wins including the defeat of Five Nations champions England, and the double over Queensland, it was already New South Wales's most successful season. The opportunity to finish off in the most triumphant manner was grabbed with both hands. Nick Farr-Jones, David Campese, Willie Ofahengaue, Simon Poidevin and company produced a stunning collective performance of almost

The Llewellyn brothers fail to stop Tim Gavin scoring for Australia.

clinical perfection. Seldom, if ever, has a team approached this level of total rugby. No more than four forwards were involved in securing the loose ball. It was simple – win it or kill it. The front-row men Daly, Kearns and McKenzie then took it in turns to batter the Welsh midfield. Grid-iron-style quarter-back Farr-Jones pinpointed his passes, Campese ran in five tries and the rest of the team added a further seven.

The rest of the tour was academic and the win at Rockhampton against Queensland Country District of no consequence. The sole aim of the final game, the Test against Australia, was to avoid an even greater drubbing than that experienced the previous Sunday. That aim at least was accomplished – but to no great satisfaction.

In the most cruel way possible 20 years of Welsh Rugby Union mismanagement had finally been exposed. Some of the young talent laid bare by such an experience may never recover, and without urgent surgery neither will Welsh rugby.

PREVIEW OF THE SEASON
1991/92

THE FIVE NATIONS CHAMPIONSHIP
by BILL McLAREN

Those who reckon that the glamour of the World Cup will dilute interest in the 1992 Five Nations Championship hardly take into account the particular attraction of each Championship campaign, a Championship that is the envy of the rugby-playing world and also one that carries with it the coveted Grand Slam, Triple Crown, Calcutta Cup and the Digital Millennium Trophy for which Ireland and England have a perpetual challenge.

Whatever happens in the World Cup the Championship will be contested with all its customary zeal, aggression, pride, passion and hopefully skill and adventurism. Although the title of World Champions represents the summit of achievement, all five contestants will be pulling out all the stops with the aim of being declared European Champions of 1992.

Martin Bayfield, understudy to Wade Dooley.

The campaign is likely to be dominated, as much by who may not be playing as by who will, because some famous personalities who have made a special mark in previous Championships are coming to the end of their international careers and may well not come to the starting block this time. If so, that could represent a serious loss to the countries concerned. It could mean a lot to England, the reigning champions, for example, if a section of their vaunted tight-five forwards have to be replaced. It is hard to imagine an England pack without those twin control towers, Wade Dooley and Paul Ackford, in their engine room. Dooley will be 34 at the start of the Championship and Ackford 33. They have seen a lot of service together and have experienced the peak of achievement as British Lions locks in the successful Test series in Australia in 1989 and as England's Grand Slam boilerhouse last season. There is no shortage of young, outsize locks in England. Martin Bayfield (Bedford) looked like an heir apparent when chosen for the tour of Australia and Fiji during the summer. He is 6ft 10in and 18 stones. That is even bigger than Dooley! There is, too, another young giant in the wings, Anthony Copsey, who has been learning the engine-room trade with Llanelli and getting some handy advice from that seasoned tutor, Phil May. But it takes time to forge an Ackford-Dooley quality partnership. England also have owed much to the sapping scrummage style of Jeff Probyn (Wasps) who was 35 in April. He too would be difficult to replace.

Even so, England will still be the team to beat because they never have many problems in creating a dependable set-piece supply and they can call on a back division ideally equipped to play to whatever style they deem the more profitable. They won the Grand Slam last season with a series of clinical displays based on eliminating error and risk but it hurt them a bit that, as champions, they scored only five tries, one less than Scotland recorded in their Grand Slam in 1990. One will be surprised if, having achieved their goal last season, England do not reach out this time for a more attractive pattern of play with more width than they sought last time. They demonstrated against Wales and France in 1990 that, given the set-piece platform, they are capable of total rugby of the very highest quality.

Tony Copsey (left) with his mentor Phil May (right) in action for Llanelli against Neath.

It is a sad thought that we may have seen the last of that remarkable French full back Serge Blanco, who was reckoned to have played his last Championship international at Parc des Princes when France beat Wales by 36-3 last March. Blanco has meant so much to France since his first cap against South Africa in 1980, apart from his 34 tries, that it is hard to imagine the French being quite the same force without him. He will be 33 when the Championship starts. Of course you never can tell with those ageing rugby stars. They are like retired actors who get a wee sniff of the greasepaint again and decide to have another shot! France's World Cup squad included Jean-Claude Sadourny (Colomiers) as Blanco's understudy and there is also Jean-Baptiste Lafond (Racing Club) who started out as a full back in a drop-goal début

The versatile Jean-Baptiste Lafond acts as scrum-half to feed the Barbarian backs.

against Australia in 1983 but has played most of his internationals as a wing. Lafond certainly possesses that quality of intuitive adventurism that has so marked Blanco's career. France still will field a class back division with perhaps the one problem position being scrum-half. Pierre Berbizier was left out of their World Cup squad, having won 56 caps and been captain 13 times, but the 22-year-old Fabien Galthié (Colomiers) didn't exactly set the heather on fire against the Romanians in June and, although sevens is an entirely different game to fifteens, the superb form of Aubin Hueber (Lourdes) as captain of the winning French Barbarians seven at the Ulster tournament in May suggested that he may yet add to the two caps won against Australia and New Zealand in 1990, as understudy to Henri Sanz (Narbonne). The French pack is sure to be formidable. They played five new forward caps against Romania who were very secure in the set pieces and, eventually, very impressive in close-passing forays. They have to decide on a regular lock partner for that mighty force, Olivier Roumat (Dax), and it will be fascinating to see if Eric Champ, back in business and in favour, can gain preference over the explosive Laurent Cabannes (Racing Club) and Xavier Blond, of the shorter fuse, also from the Racing Club.

Scotland have based so much of their recent success on the mobility and cohesiveness of their breakaway trio that any change has to occasion some concern, although their tour to North America in May enabled to them pencil in two young club number 8 forwards as possible cap flankers, Stuart Reid (Boroughmuir) and Ron Kirkpatrick (Jed-Forest). Reid's parents were born in Hawick but set up a knitwear business in Kendal. The lad has toured with England Schools out of St Bee's and was playing for Vale of Lune when called to Scotland's colours in the Under-21 side. He seems a front runner as a cap contender should the old firm of John Jeffrey, Derek White and Derek Turnbull break up. Kirkpatrick has formed a profitable liaison with Gary Armstrong in the Jed-Forest side and has all the makings of a very good player except perhaps in the realm of pure physique. He has acute positional instinct and excels as an attack generator. Scotland would feel some concern if David Sole could not come to the starting-gate because there seems no ready-made loose-head prop of genuine international calibre although the third of the Milne brothers, David, would do a job and there have been times when Grant Wilson (Boroughmuir) has hinted at introducing that necessary aggression into his play that would fit him out for cap status. Indeed Scotland may one day field two Boroughmuir props because their tight head, Peter Wright, a tough, young blacksmith, has the right attitude and ambition. It has done those Boroughmuir props no harm either that the former Grand Slam captain, Jim Aitken, has been helping former Lions full back, Bruce Hay, with the preparation of the Meggetland squad. The North American tour also brought plus marks for a slim, wiry and very quick left wing, Mark Moncrieff (Gala), a tidy scrum half with quick hands, Andy Nicol (Dundee High School FP) who pressed Greig Oliver (Hawick) hard for the Test spot, and for the former Cambridge University lock, Andrew McDonald, who is 6ft 8in and 18 stones, and could form an interesting blend with the slimmer 'Doddie' Weir (Melrose) who stands up well to the buffeting in line-out action. The national selectors also believe that the Glasgow High-Kelvinside lock, Alan Watt, will adapt to the tight-head role even at 6ft 5in and 20 stones.

Scots traditionally are loathe to part with seasoned warriors and will want to hold on to their World Cup men for as long as possible. It takes quite a long time to fashion a genuine international player. Scotland, too, are most likely to base their strategy on their pivot five although hopefully they will reach out for a more expansive repertoire. In which regard they will be hoping for a higher quality of creativity from their midfield and a continuance of that aggressive and copybook tackling from the entire side that has been such a feature of their pattern almost since internationals began.

There will be keen disappointment in Ireland if their squad does not make a strong bid for Championship honours, for their back division made folk sit up and take notice last season and indications are that the squad will be the fittest ever fielded by Ireland. It remains to be seen whether their tight five have the requisite power and acumen to provide the necessary bulwark and if Neil Francis, potentially an inspiring figure, can blow hot all the time instead of hot and cold as he is wont to do. Certainly, with Pat O'Hara (Sunday's Well) and Philip Matthews (Wanderers) restored after injury and full of vim and vigour again, Ireland should be well fitted out for ball-winning at breakdown, for fringe defence and for loose-forward

The Irish will be hoping for more of the same from Simon Geoghegan.

support-play. The switch by Brian Smith to rugby league in Australia left Ireland short of a ready-made stand-off with international experience although if Ralph Keyes (Cork Constitution) has overcome injury problems he might well inherit that crucial role. Keyes has played some very good games for Munster. Ireland too must unearth a dependable goal-kicker perhaps from the Ollie Campbell school of goal-kicking improvement. The former Lions stand-off has been giving the benefit of his place-kicking expertise to several young hopefuls. Not only the Irish will be looking forward to seeing Ireland's adventurous back division in action again and especially that blond bullet Simon Geoghegan who so took the Championship by storm last season with tries against Wales, England and Scotland.

As for Wales, they certainly didn't lack courage in undertaking a six-match tour of Australia in June and July against Australians already well into their preparations for the World Cup. That was the kind of tour, with especially demanding contests against Queensland, Sydney and Australia, that could have sent Welsh confidence soaring but as it happened only added to the gloom of recent events.

Despite this shattering experience Wales could still have one of the most exciting back divisions in the 1992 Championship even though that eccentric swashbuckler Mark Ring wasn't chosen for the tour down under. There have been high hopes for Luc Evans of Llanelli as understudy to Paul Thorburn (Neath). Evans is something of an adventurous last line who could spark off that nippy back division. But rugby union is essentially about ball winning and, whilst a breakaway trio from Martyn Morris, Richard Webster, Ritchie Collins, Emyr Lewis, and Phil Davies holds out much promise, the first priority has to be a settled tight five with the necessary ballast and physique to provide a solid scrummage and productive line-out. Hopefully for Wales, Gareth Llewellyn (Neath) and Richard Goodey (Pontypool) will mount a strong challenge for boilerhouse places. Given that, Wales could be quite a force provided there is consistency in selection. It was no help to the Welsh cause that from the start of their tour of Namibia in June 1990 to the end of the 1991 Championship no fewer that 33 players were capped. A lot will depend on how Wales fare in the World Cup under the temporary guidance of Alan Davies.

Richard Goodey (extreme left) watches his Pontypool scrum-half Ceri Jonathan feed the ball to the backs during the Schweppes Cup semi-final against Swansea.

France will enter the Championship 'cold' as they are not involved on the opening day, January 18. As they travel to Cardiff a fortnight later they might reason that that might be an ideal warmer for what could be the crunch match of the Championship, France v England in Paris on February 15. England have no game on the last day so the reigning champions may have the title stowed away by the time France play Ireland in Paris and Wales meet Scotland

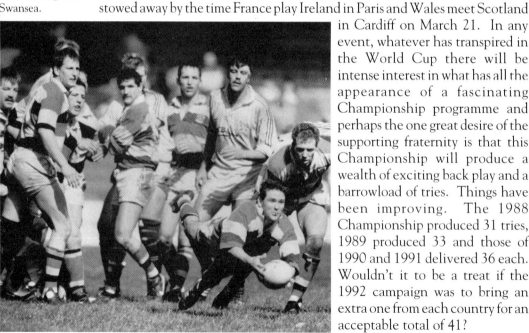

in Cardiff on March 21. In any event, whatever has transpired in the World Cup there will be intense interest in what has all the appearance of a fascinating Championship programme and perhaps the one great desire of the supporting fraternity is that this Championship will produce a wealth of exciting back play and a barrowload of tries. Things have been improving. The 1988 Championship produced 31 tries, 1989 produced 33 and those of 1990 and 1991 delivered 36 each. Wouldn't it to be a treat if the 1992 campaign was to bring an extra one from each country for an acceptable total of 41?

KEY PLAYERS

ENGLAND

WILL CARLING

DEAN RICHARDS

After a meteoric rise to the top, Will Carling won his first cap in 1988 against France at the age of 22 and he went on to become Captain that same year against Australia. He began his representative career when he had two seasons in the England Schools side in 1983 and 1984, captaining them in his second season. He played for Durham University and the Army before winning an England 'B' Cap against France in 1987. Within twelve months he won his first full cap for England and has been first choice ever since, although he missed the Romanian match in the spring of 1989 because of a leg injury which also forced him to drop out of the British Lions tour to Australia that summer. He is a very fast, strong, aggressive runner with a keen eye for a gap and a fierce determination when the line is in his sights. In 1990 he scored tries against France and Wales in the Five Nations Championship with some powerful running. He has a good defensive record for England and along with Rob Andrew and Jeremy Guscott, the English midfield is hard to penetrate. By the end of the 1991 Championship, he had led England a total of 17 times which means he is well on the way to Bill Beaumont's record of 21. At his best, he is an inspirational player who should captain England for several more seasons and could well captain the 1993 British Lions.

The great strength of the England Grand Slam side has been the tremendously consistent form of their pack, and the focal point of that thundering power has been Dean Richards. He has been the apex of their whole forward thrust. It was no surprise to anyone that he was chosen as the 1991 Whitbread Rugby World Player of the Year. He began his representative career ten years ago when he played for England Schools at lock forward and he played for England Under 23 before winning his first cap against Ireland at Twickenham in 1986. He had an outstanding tour with the 1989 British Lions in Australia where he played in all three Tests and made a major contribution to the Lions winning the series. He missed the 1990 season through injury and many English supporters felt strongly that if Dean had played in the 1990 Calcutta Cup game England would have won the Grand Slam that season as well. A good line-out player and a strong scrummager, he has very good hands and is particularly good at reading the game. He has an uncanny knack of always being in the right place at the right time and invariably doing the right thing. He is one of those few number 8 forwards who is just as good in defence as he is in attack and he would be regarded generally as the most important member of the England pack.

FRANCE

LAURENT CABANNES

OLIVIER ROUMAT

The tremendous current strength of the top club in Paris, the famous Racing Club de France, is exemplified by the fact that their exciting flanker, Laurent Cabannes, is just one of five players in the French national side at the moment. Cabannes began his representative career when he played for France 'B' in their narrow win over Wales 'B' in 1988. He missed most of the next season through injury but his outstanding performances at club level helped him to win his first full cap for France when he came on as a replacement for Benazzi in the second Test against New Zealand in Paris in November 1990 at the age of 26. He played in all four Internationals in the Five Nations Championship in 1991 and is now firmly established in the revamped and revitalised French pack. When the career of Jean-Pierre Rives ended in 1984, France struggled to find an open-side flanker with similar flamboyant skills and several players have come and gone in this crucial position. At last France are poised to recapture the glory days of Rives. Cabannes is fast, strong, has good hands and is a creative player in the best tradition of French forwards. Perpetual-motion Cabannes can take France back to the top in the next couple of seasons.

The French have produced a host of great forwards in the past fifteen years in almost every position except at lock. They have had to rely instead on hard grafting journeymen like Palmié and Imbernon in the Seventies and Condom, Haget and Lorieux in the Eighties. Olivier Roumat has changed all that. 6ft 6in and well over 17 stone, he is the best line-out jumper in French rugby and potentially their best lock forward for the past two decades. Whilst he has all the raw attributes of an international lock – a great jumper and solid scrummager – he has a lot more to offer. As befits a player who has been chosen to play for France at flank forward and also at number 8 at the start of his representative career, he is the ideal athletic type of forward who is just as formidable in open play as he is in the set-pieces. He won his first cap at the age of 24 against New Zealand in 1989 and after several caps in the back row he switched with dramatic success to lock, the position he plays for his club side, Dax. After so many years of struggling to win good, clean line-out possession, Roumat has added another dimension to French forward play without sacrificing any of the more traditional skills which have made France such feared opponents. After a couple of disappointing seasons, France looks formidable once more.

Pontypool scrum-half Ceri Jonathan threatens to halt Swansea's Kevin Price in the Schweppes Welsh Cup semi-final.

Bath entertain
Romania at the
Recreation
Ground.

A wry smile from All Black Steve McDowell during half-time in the New Zealanders' match against Cuyo on their Argentinian tour. On his left newcomer Paul Henderson soaks up the atmosphere of an All Black tour.

David Pears
prepares to pass to
John Buckton
during the England
'B' match against
the Emerging
Wallabies.

Northampton
enjoy their
Pilkington Cup
semi-final victory
over Orrell – sweet
revenge after their
humiliation by the
same opponents in
their Courage
League match
earlier in the
season .

The final whistle, and Bradford Salem are winners of the Provincial Insurance Cup after defeating Bicester.

Auckland (in blue and white), on their way to retaining the Ranfurly Shield yet again, this time the challengers are Bay of Plenty. Here Michael Jones (left) stems an attack while Robin Brooke – younger brother of Zinzan and probably a future All Black – stands by to help if needed.

Line-out action in the Pilkington Cup final between Harlequins and Northampton.

The fanatical
Cornish
supporters had
plenty to
celebrate after
their extra-time
victory over
Yorkshire in the
ADT County
Championship
final.

IRELAND

ROB SAUNDERS

SIMON GEOGHEGAN

Representative honours have come thick and fast for Rob Saunders who has made a tremendous impact on the international scene in a very short time. He captained Ulster Schools in 1987 and toured Australia before going on to captain the Irish Students, the Irish Universities, the Ireland Under-21 side and Ireland 'B'. Confirming his reputation as an outstanding scrum-half and captain, he went on to join that very rare band of men who captained their country when winning their first cap. A natural leader, he deserved a great deal of the credit for Ireland's spirited performance in defeat against France. A good half-back partnership is essential for success at international level and at least Ireland has solved half the problem. Saunders has an instinctive feel for the game, he has a crisp, accurate pass, he kicks well and is very good at linking with this loose forwards. Above all, he has quick hands which means he is able to work minor miracles with poor possession and often manages to make something out of nothing. He is already established as captain at a remarkable young age – he is only 23 now – and, despite some disappointing results in the 1991 Five Nations Championship, Ireland played some very good rugby and can look forward with great optimism to the new domestic season.

Very few players have exploded on to the international scene with quite such devastating effect as Simon Geoghegan achieved at the age of 22 in 1991. Educated in England but with an Irish father he began his representative career playing for Irish Students against USA in Dublin 1990. The following season he was very quick to impress the Irish selectors with excellent performances for Ireland Under 25, Connacht and Ireland 'B' when they played against the Argentine touring team. He scored some spectacular tries in these matches and continued his good form with Connacht in the build-up to the Five Nations Championship. He came into the Irish squad when Keith Crossan was injured and won his first full cap against France. He played in all four Internationals in 1991 and scored memorable tries against Wales, England and Scotland. Apart from Trevor Ringland in the mid-Eighties, it has been a long time since an Irish wing scored three International tries in a domestic season. He is equally forthright in attack and defence and he has been an inspiration to his colleagues. Like the great All Black wing, John Kirwan, Simon is a very potent mixture of raw strength, power and blistering pace, backed up by a fierce competitive determination. He looks sure to have a very bright future and was a deserving winner of the Whitbread Rugby World Most Promising Player of the Year Award.

SCOTLAND

TONY STANGER

JOHN JEFFREY

After beginning his representative career playing in the centre for Scottish schools he switched to the right wing when he began his senior club career with Hawick. He soon became a regular in the South of Scotland team in the District championship and at the age of 21 won his first full cap against Fiji at Murrayfield in 1989. He scored two tries in that match and by the end of the 1991 Five Nations Championship he had scored 10 tries in total including three in one match against Romania and the famous try against England at Murrayfield in the 1990 Calcutta Cup match which helped Scotland complete their second Grand Slam in six years. He toured Japan with Scotland in 1989 and notched up three tries in the two matches he played but he would probably be more pleased with the try he scored for Scotland at Auckland in the second Test against New Zealand in 1990 when Scotland came desperately close to recording their first ever win over the All Blacks leading 18-15 until the closing minutes. He is a very powerful, abrasive runner in the John Kirwan mould and at 6ft 2in and nearly 14 stone he takes some stopping. After the triumphs of 1990, he made the most of fewer opportunities in 1991 but, if the pack win their share of possession, Tony Stanger is bound to score many more tries for Scotland and, at his present rate of progress, he may well have Ian Smith's 58 year old record of 24 tries in his sights well before the 1995 World Cup.

A regular member of the Scottish pack for seven seasons, John Jeffrey won his first full cap against Australia at Murrayfield in 1984 just eight months after the Scottish Grand Slam that year. By the end of the 1991 Five Nations Championship he had become the most capped Scottish back-row forward in history with 35 caps and he holds the try-scoring record for a Scottish forward with nine tries. He scored two in 1986, against Wales and Romania, and the following year he scored three in the win over Romania and one each against Wales and Zimbabwe. He has also scored tries against England and Ireland. He was a key player in the Scotland side in the 1987 World Cup and was crucial to the Grand Slam success of 1990 when he combined with Finlay Calder and Derek White to produce the most formidable back-row trio in the Championship. He gained valuable experience with the British Lions in 1989 even though he did not play in a Test and he is now playing the best rugby of his career. He is a very useful line-out jumper, a strong scrummager and in the open he is now just as good going back in defence as he is going forward in attack. He is a natural footballer with tremendous speed for a big forward, a powerful runner and a good support player with safe hands. He has made his reputation as a devastating attacking player but he has developed in recent seasons into the complete all-round flanker.

WALES

PHIL DAVIES

SCOTT GIBBS

After playing for Welsh Schools and Welsh Youth, he began his senior career with Llanelli in 1982. He won his first cap for Wales against England at Cardiff in 1985 and was a regular member of the side right through to the World Cup in 1987. He played all his early international rugby at number 8 but when he was recalled to the team in 1989 he was chosen at lock. He helped Wales to win the Triple Crown that season but since then Wales have suffered a dramatic slump. Erratic selection has meant he has been in and out of the side in the past year, but under the new regime he looks sure to play a major role in masterminding the Welsh resurgence. He is the one real world class forward in Wales and it is essential the pack is built around his formidable presence. An outstanding natural footballer he is equally good in attack and defence, and the fact that he has played for Wales at number 8, lock and flanker shows his great versatility. Still only 27 years of age at the start of this season he is already by far the most experienced forward in the Welsh side with 29 Internationals behind him before the 1991 World Cup. After the various disappointing results in 1991 in the Five Nations Championship and the record defeats in Australia against New South Wales and Australia his experience, all-round skill and leadership qualities will be crucial as Wales try to recapture the glory days of the Seventies.

It is hard enough for a young player to make an impact in his first season of international rugby in ordinary circumstances but even more so in a losing team behind a beaten pack. Full credit then to Scott Gibbs who exploded on to the international scene in 1991 and very quickly established himself as the best back in Welsh rugby. He was captain of Wales Youth the previous season with victories against England and Italy. He rapidly caught the eye of the Welsh selectors and rocketed from the Wales 'B' squad to his first full cap at the age of 19 against England at Cardiff. He made the transition to the highest level with amazing ease and had the confidence and the skill to make his mark in all four matches in the Championship. He is an elusive runner with the ability to cut back inside and accelerate out again to link up with his wings, and the priceless talent to make an outside break in the classical tradition of great Welsh threequarters. He is also strong enough to ride most tackles and keep the ball in play. On many occasions he managed to make something out of nothing in attack whilst ensuring he was fully committed to his defensive role in midfield. Wales had to do more than their fair share of tackling in 1991 and Scott Gibbs was not found wanting. He is unquestionably the most exciting talent to hit the Welsh team for some time and he has the potential to inspire all those around him and help Wales recapture past glories in the near future.

FIXTURES
1991-92

August 1991

Sat	31st	Romania v Scotland

September 1991

Sun	1st	England Under 21 v Belgium
Tue	3rd	Combined London Old Boys v Soviet Union
Wed	4th	Wales v France
Sat	7th	An England XV v Soviet Union
		Scotland v Barbarians
Tue	10th	Cork Constitution v Barbarians
Thu	12th	Old Wesley v Barbarians
Sat	14th	An England XV v Gloucester
		London & SE Division v Munster
		South of Scotland v Glasgow
		Edinburgh v Anglo Scots
		North & Midlands v President's XV
Sat	21st	An England XV v England Students
		Pilkington Cup 1st Round
		Provincial Insurance Cup 1st Round
		Schweppes Welsh Cup 1st Round
		Anglo Scots v President's XV
		South of Scotland v Edinburgh
		Glasgow v North & Midlands

October 1991

Thu	3rd	England v New Zealand (World Cup)
Fri	4th	Australia v Argentina (World Cup)
		France v Romania (World Cup)
Sat	5th	Scotland v Japan (World Cup)
		Italy v USA (World Cup)
		Fiji v Canada (World Cup)
		London v South
		Midlands v North
		ADT County Championship matches
		Provincial Insurance Cup 2nd Round
Sun	6th	Ireland v Zimbabwe (World Cup)
		Wales v Western Samoa (World Cup)
Tue	8th	New Zealand v USA (World Cup)
		France v Fiji (World Cup)

		England v Italy (World Cup)
Wed	9th	Ireland v Japan (World Cup)
		Scotland v Zimbabwe (World Cup)
		Australia v W Samoa (World Cup)
		Wales v Argentina (World Cup)
		Canada v Romania (World Cup)
Fri	11th	England v USA (World Cup)
Sat	12th	Scotland v Ireland (World Cup)
		Wales v Australia (World Cup)
		Fiji v Romania (World Cup)
		North v London
		South West v Midlands
		ADT County Championship matches
Sun	13th	New Zealand v Italy (World Cup)
		Argentina v W Samoa (World Cup)
		France v Canada (World Cup)
Mon	14th	Zimbabwe v Japan (World Cup)
Sat	19th	World Cup Quarter-finals
		Midlands v London
		South West v North
		Provincial Insurance Cup 3rd Round
		Schweppes Welsh Cup 2nd Round
Sun	20th	World Cup Quarter-finals
Wed	23rd	Ireland Under 21 v England Under 21
Sat	26th	World Cup Semi-final
Sun	27th	World Cup Semi-final
Wed	30th	World Cup Third Place Play-off

November 1991

Sat	2nd	World Cup Final
Wed	6th	Oxford Univ v Major Stanley's XV
		Newport v Barbarians
Sat	9th	Pilkington Cup 2nd Round
		Provincial Insurance Cup 4th Round
		McEwan's National Leagues (1)
		Heineken Leagues (1)
		Insurance Corp All Ireland Leagues (1)
Sat	16th	Courage Leagues (1)
		McEwan's National Leagues (2)
		Heineken Leagues (2)

Sat	16th	Insurance Corp All Ireland Leagues (2)
		Schweppes Welsh Cup 3rd Round
Sat	23rd	Courage Leagues (2)
		McEwan's National Leagues (3)
		Heineken's Leagues (3)
		Insurance Corp All Ireland Leagues (3)
Wed	27th	Camb Univ v M.R. Steele-Bodger's XV
Sat	30th	Pilkington Cup 3rd Round
		Provincial Insurance Cup 3rd Round
		MeEwan's National Leagues (4)
		Heineken Leagues (4)
		Insurance Corp All Ireland Leagues (4)

December 1991

Sat	7th	Courage Leagues (3)
		McEwan's National Leagues (5)
		Heineken Leagues (5)
		Connacht v Munster
		Leinster v Ulster
Tue	10th	Oxford Univ v Cambridge Univ
Sat	14th	County Colts Cup Final
		Courage Leagues (4)
		McEwan's National Leagues (6)
		Heineken Leagues (6)
		Leinster v Connacht
		Ulster v Munster
Sat	21st	Courage Leagues (5)
		McEwan's National Leagues (7)
		Schweppes Welsh Cup 4th Round
		Munster v Leinster
		Connacht v Ulster
		Heineken Leagues (7)
Sun	29th	Leicester v Barbarians
		Scotland 'B' v Ireland 'B'

January 1992

Sat	4th	Courage Leagues (6)
		Heineken Leagues (8)
		Insurance Corp All Ireland Leagues (5)
		Scotland International Trial
Sat	11th	Courage Leagues (7)
		McEwan's National Leagues (8)
		Heineken Leagues (9)
Fri	17th	Scotland Students v England Students
Sat	18th	Scotland v England
		Ireland v Wales
Sun	19th	Spain 'B' v England 'B'

Sat	25th	Pilkington Cup 4th Round
		Schweppes Welsh Cup 5th Round
		Provincial Insurance Cup 6th Round
		Insurance Corp All Ireland Leagues (6)
		McEwan's National Leagues (9)
Fri	31st	England Students v Ireland Students
		England 'B' v Ireland 'B'

February 1992

Sat	1st	England v Ireland
		Wales v France
Sun	2nd	France 'B' v Scotland 'B'
Sat	8th	Courage Leagues (8)
		McEwan's National Leagues (10)
		Heineken Leagues (10)
		Insurance Corp All Ireland Leagues (7)
Fri	14th	France Students v England Students
Sat	15th	France v England
		Ireland v Scotland
		France 'B' v England 'B'
		Heineken Leagues (11)
Sat	22nd	Pilkington Cup Quarter-finals
		Schweppes Welsh Cup 6th Round
		McEwan's National Leagues (11)
		Provincial Insurance Cup Quarter-finals
		Insurance Corp All Ireland Leagues (8)
Sat	29th	Courage Leagues (9)
		McEwan's National Leagues (12)
		Heineken Leagues (12)
		Insurance Corp All Ireland Leagues (9) and Round Robin play-offs Ireland

March 1992

Fri	6th	England Students v Wales Students
Sat	7th	England v Wales
		Scotland v France
		Insurance Corp All Ireland Leagues Round Robin play-offs
		Italy 'B' v England 'B'
Wed	11th	East Midlands v Barbarians
Sat	14th	Courage Leagues (10)
		McEwan's National Leagues (13)
		Heineken Leagues (13)
		Insurance Corp All Ireland Leagues Round Robin play-offs
		Italy Juniors v England Colts

Wed 18th UAU Final
Sat 21st France v Ireland
Wales v Scotland
Royal Navy v Army
ADT County Championship Semi-
finals
Provincial Insurance Cup Semi-finals
Sat 28th Courage Leagues (11)
Royal Navy v Royal Air Force
McEwan's National Leagues (spare
date)
Heineken Leagues (14)

April 1992
Sat 4th Pilkington Cup Semi-finals
Provincial Insurance Cup Final
Daily Mail Schools Under 15 and
Under 18 Finals
Wales Youth v England Colts
Schweppes Welsh Cup Quarter-finals
Gala Sevens
Hong Kong Sevens
Sun 5th Hong Kong Sevens
Sat 11th Courage Leagues (12)
Heineken Leagues (15)
Army v Royal Air Force
Scotland v England (18 Group)
England Colts v Scotland Under 19
Melrose Sevens
Wed 15th England v Ireland (18 Group)
Sat 18th ADT County Championship Final
Under 21 County Championship Final
France v England (18 Group)
Heineken Leagues (16)
Cardiff v Barbarians
Hawick Sevens
Mon 20th Swansea v Barbarians
Sat 25th Courage Leagues (13)
England Colts v France Colts
England v Wales (18 Group)
Wales v England (16 Group)
Heineken Leagues (17)
Jed-Forest Sevens
Irish Provincial Cup Finals
(provisional)

May 1992
Sat 2nd Pilkington Cup Final
Schweppes Welsh Cup Semi-finals
Langholm Sevens
Sat 9th Middlesex Sevens Finals
Heineken Leagues (18)
Sat 16th Schweppes Welsh Cup Final

REVIEW OF THE SEASON
1990/91

CLUB SCENE

BATH STILL SET THE PACE
by Nick Cain

Mike Slemen read the form from 'the off'. After seeing his callow Liverpool St Helens side clinically taken apart by Bath (46-3) on the first league weekend of the season the England 'B' coach declared; "I'm not that disappointed by the result. Bath are by far the best side around."

As they strode on to reclaim the Courage Clubs Championship title they covet as their birthright, Bath left numerous opponents – not least Rosslyn Park (45-21) and Saracens (49-6) – nodding in agreement with Slemen's autumn appraisal: "I was amazed at how they make the right decisions all the time. We were never going to beat Bath at this stage of our development," concluded Slemen.

Unfortunately for Liverpool St Helens the First Division is no nursery for young flowers. Their lightweight pack was never able to secure enough possession and they were severely embarrassed by the other members of England's club elite – Wasps, Harlequins and Leicester. They finished without a win in twelve outings and were relegated to the Second Division after only a few months back at the top level.

That Bath remain pre-eminent in the England game is a tribute to a professionalism which has few equals in club rugby at home or abroad. The price you pay, however, for a championship spanning only twelve games is that for much of the season the title chase was on for half-a-dozen clubs.

The Bath star looked as if it was on the wane when defeat by Leicester in the 3rd Round of the Pilkington Cup was compounded by a series of less than authoritative performances at the start of the new year. This culminated in their 16-15 reverse at the hands of erstwhile champions Wasps, who inflicted Bath's first league defeat at the Recreation Ground thanks to a remarkable injury time try by Fran Clough.

With a demanding itinerary, including away visits to Gloucester, Nottingham and Saracens still outstanding, Bath appeared to have been rumbled. But, having already weathered an early season internal dispute which led to the resignation of coaches Tom Hudson and Dave Robson, we should have known that they were made of sterner stuff. Never one to duck a challenge, chief coach Jack Rowell took up the mantle. Rowell, an astute tactician, motivator and man-manager who is arguably the club's most important asset, has always marshalled his resources with great care.

As a consequence the departure to Harlequins of a player as crucial to Bath's success as Simon Halliday did not detonate their title aspirations. The reserve strength so carefully cultivated by Rowell came into its own. By the end of the league campaign centre Phil de Glanville, winger Adedayo Adebayo, lock Martin Haag, number 8 Steve Ojomoh and prop Martin Crane had made their marks. The integration of England full back Jon Webb following his departure from Bristol was another coup, while careful nurturing has seen the talented Audley Lumsden make a remarkable recovery from a broken neck.

With first Orrell and then Wasps in place to exploit any Bath slip-ups they had the added pressure of having to make the home run away from home. But Stuart Barnes's boys were not to be denied. The crucial encounter came at Kingsholm where Bath showed their mettle to withstand a late Gloucester surge and carry the day 18-15.

Skipper Barnes, who has now stepped down after three years in charge, won ringing plaudits from his coach. "Stuart kept the side on course throughout the season," said Rowell, "and was instrumental in helping us win those crucial last away games at Gloucester and Nottingham."

In their thorough way, Bath will no doubt have noted that the league system retains no residual respect for famous names or past deeds. London Welsh, who managed to arrest the slide by finishing third in the Fourth Division South, have discovered this the hard way. So have Moseley, although they intend to make their fall from grace less severe than that of the Welsh, as they take the drop to the second tier alongside Liverpool St Helens.

The demise of the Midlanders encapsulates the demands of the New Order. Consistency is everything and failure to lay the foundations in terms of internal club organisation is costly. Bath, despite wrangles between the playing administration and the committee, were streets ahead of the rest: now the rest are trying to catch up.

Bath's Pilkington Cup hopes are ended by Leicester.

The most revolutionary aspect of the domestic season was the growth of a new breed: paid directors of coaching. Having appointed their own technical administrator in 1970 the RFU gave Northampton the nod to follow suit twenty years later. They set the pace by appointing Barrie Corless and by the end of 1990, Leicester, Bristol, Newcastle Gosforth, London Welsh and Newbury all had paid directors of coaching on salaries of £20,000 to £30,000 p.a.

In one of those fudges for which the administrators of the game are famous, directors currently may not coach their teams – although they may coach coaches and players on other than a team basis. The RFU will need to re-initial itself KGB if it intends to police that one!

The quest for success under the New Order also highlights the struggle for survival. The axe has already fallen on a number of coaches, while some of the army of unpaid committee men who sustain the club system are bound to become disaffected by the prospect of a director being paid handsomely for jobs they always considered a labour of love.

Of the coaches the most glaring dismissal was that of Paul Bryant after taking Northampton to their first-ever Cup final. Despite giving the all-star Harlequins a fright in front of a 50,000 crowd at Twickenham before succumbing 25-13, and despite maintaining their newly won First Division status, Bryant was judged by a more exacting yardstick. His side was inconsistent and without Wayne Shelford's inspiration was capable of plumbing the depths as Orrell (60-0) and Rosslyn Park (48-0) demonstrated.

It was predicted that the introduction of leagues would change English rugby. It has. Moseley coach Derek Nutt – who survived a mid-season no-confidence vote only to be told that the club would be appointing a paid administrator – reflects on his relegation season thus: "We set out to put Moseley back together, i.e. to play attractive 15-man rugby. In my view it is a three-year task which we are only two years into. It'll be very disappointing if we can't continue but we're now very close to pro football in the way clubs are run, so we live with those pressures.

"We've a young side and I'm confident we'll come straight back up if we play as we have this season. I'm that confident of our ability. Certainly I saw nothing in Rugby that suggests they'll stay up. What worries me is cheque book rugby. If someone's prepared to pay £100 per match, I can't side with that; it's not rugby.

"But seeing as we're appointing a paid administrator I'm happy to do whatever they want me to. If it's pulling a few pints, so be it. I'm a club man through and through."

MUNSTER CLUBS DOMINATE
by Sean Diffley

Last season, at last, the Irish joined the comity of rugby nations and commenced their first ever national competition, the All Ireland League. Hitherto the Irish were the only major rugby country which had no national event to hone the edges of the leading club players. Instead competitive rugby was confined to the four provincial leagues and cups, interspersed with undemanding friendlies which took up most of the season.

The IRFU, fully aware of the void in the game in Ireland, did not find it easy to introduce the national competition. Many of the clubs found it difficult to jettison their traditional niches in the Irish game, viewing the idea of promotion and relegation as a bit much to swallow. But IRFU patience paid off eventually and the All Ireland League came to fruition with the top 19 of the 48 senior clubs taking part in two divisions. Based on provincial league results over the previous few seasons the clubs were divided into nine in Division One and ten in Division Two.

The feature of the inaugural season was the wholehearted enthusiasm of the Munster clubs in particular. The forecasts had Wanderers and Lansdowne in Leinster and Ballymena in Ulster as the likely battlers for first division honours. In fact it was the Munster clubs which dominated, Cork Constitution winning the title after a memorable battle with Garryowen in Limerick on the final day of the League. It was a dream start with first and second placings depending on the last tie a virtual 'cup final', rather than a league tie.

Three of the top four in the table were Munster clubs, only Lansdowne intervening in third place as Constitution, Garryowen and Shannon dominated. And the shock was that Wanderers found themselves relegated, with Malone.

Up to Division One went Young Munster (to give Limerick city its third Division One side for the 1991/92 season) and Old Wesley. The Munster success was based on the sheer enthusiasm and passion of their clubs. Special trains were chartered for the away matches. Supporters travelled in their hundreds, relegating forever to history the image of Irish club rugby as something to be watched only by two men and a dog. The atmosphere everywhere was tremendous with the AIL getting superb coverage in the media.

The big question now is – will lightning strike twice? Can the standards and the interest be maintained? Perhaps it would be a bit too much to hope for a repeat of the 1990/91 scenario. But there is every confidence among the clubs, the players and the IRFU that the AIL will be a great success, transforming the image of the club game, heightening interest for both the players and the spectators.

Over the years leading players like Fergus Slattery and Mike Gibson have pointed to the void in the Irish game. Now, it is clear, the new venture has been widely welcomed. The Irish coach, Ciaran Fitzgerald, forever a realist, is enthusiastic about the value of the AIL to the national team but he points out that it will take a few seasons before that value becomes apparent. The AIL will improve standards of play but it will not happen overnight.

For 1991/92 Division One will have Cork Constitution, Garryowen, Lansdowne, Shannon, Ballymena, Instonians, St. Mary's College, Old Wesley and Young Munster battling wholeheartedly for Constitution's title.

In Division Two the ten clubs are Wanderers, Malone, Bangor, Terenure College, Greystones, Sunday's Well, CIYMS, Blackrock College, Dolphin and Dungannon. The latter three won their places in a round-robin of the four provincial league winners. The odd side out was the Connacht League champions, Galwegians. The three relegated from division two to be replaced by the sides successful in the round robin were NIFC, Corinthians and Athlone.

The upshot of all that means that Connacht will now have no representative in the AIL. That is, of course, a matter of concern because the western province has always to fight a battle to maintain the game west of the Shannon. It has been widely suggested that in the future the round robin should be abandoned and that all four provincial winners should be automatically included in division two with four instead of three clubs being relegated.

The 1991/92 season will be the busiest in all of Irish rugby history. There are the pre-season preparations for the World Cup for the squad of 44 players which, in Irish terms, means nearly all the players of representative potential in the country. Then, the 'let down' after the World Cup in October, just a few weeks to prepare for the Five Nations Championship and, in the between, the Inter-Provincial Championship.

Connacht, with their roster of London Irish players, are viewing the elevation of London Irish to Division One of the Courage League with mixed feelings. The demands on Jim Staples, David Curtis and Simon Geoghegan will be intense, even if the IRFU have agreed that Connacht can play some of their games on Sunday when London Irish have League ties on the Saturdays.

All of which will give the London Irish Connachtmen little scope for resuscitation. But, then, few of the top players will have much time to commune with nature this season, or to stop and smell the rose. In fact, many are wondering if the demands on the players for representative events has run out of control. But this is an unusual season and, of course, the majority of senior club players will not be in demand in the higher reaches of the game. Their priorities will be concerned with AIL and the fortunes of their clubs.

This season Young Munster, with the most enthusiastic supporters in the land will be traversing Ireland by road and rail, and perhaps even flying up to Belfast. It's a far cry, this latter day sophistication, from the time they won the Bateman Cup back in 1928 and, as an old alickadoo insists, left their hotel in Dublin in single file, with each player's hand on the shoulder of the man in front "so's we wouldn't get lost". The All Ireland League, if nothing else, means that Irish club rugby is no longer travelling in single file.

Garryowen and Cork Constitution vie for supremacy at the top of the All-Ireland League.

SUCCESS AT LAST FOR BOROUGHMUIR
by Bill McLaren

It was on 30th March 1991 that the Edinburgh club, Boroughmuir, came in out of the cold and, for once, did not flatter to deceive. On that joyous day and before their own ecstatic support on their home patch at Meggetland, they scored seven tries in the 34-14 defeat of Edinburgh Wanderers to clinch Scotland's Division One championship for the first time in the 18 years of the competition.

It was a notable effort that brought much pleasure all over Edinburgh for it was only the second occasion on which one of the capital's clubs had won the coveted National League title, the previous Edinburgh winners having been Heriot's FP in 1979. This time Heriot's FP chased Boroughmuir all the way and finished runners-up, just one championship point behind.

As one of the three clubs who have never been out of Division One, the others being Heriot's FP and Hawick, Boroughmuir often have seemed to have the personnel to take them to the promised land but have been subject to such inconsistency of form and failure to reach potential, especially against some of the weaker brethren, as to have created an aura of vulnerability and a capacity for shooting themselves in the foot. Their record of having lost some 26 of 71 championship games leading up to the 1991 run-in provides the statistical evidence, although they had been runners-up in Division One to Hawick in 1977-78 and to Kelso in 1988-89. In the days of the old unofficial club championship they had been top dogs in 1955 and 1973.

This time, however, they were not to be denied. They were so well equipped in personnel as to be able to play to any style and they gave some very impressive demonstrations of the total game with a big, heavy pack capable of providing initial thrust and set-piece variety as well as blanket support whenever the ball was swung wide. They made very effective use of forwards standing off at breakdown points with the big policeman, Ken Wilson, a considerable force in the secondary drive from blind-side flanker. They also had such ballast and power in their tight five as to be able to guarantee much manicured possession from set and stoppage phases and their appraisal of when to keep it close and when to lay it back generally was sound. They had a strong scrum-half in Mike Hall who had a close liaison with his loose forwards, Wilson, Stuart Reid and Graham Drummond, all three of them having reached senior district level and Reid since having proved a resounding success on Scotland's recent tour of North America. All three of their regular front row, Grant Wilson, Barrie Brown and Peter Wright, have played for Scotland 'B' and toured with Scotland, their RAF lock, Brian Richardson, also was in North America with the national party and the other lock, Jonathan Price, has been an Edinburgh regular for several seasons. In wake of such an experienced pack, stand-off Murry Walker, who had toured with Scotland in Japan in 1989, scored 297 points including 19 tries, and one of the features of the back play was the clever choice of running angles by their international second five-eighth, Sean Lineen, who frequently thus disrupted opposing defence lines with consequent benefit to supporting colleagues among whom the captain, full back Steve Douglas, excelled in line augmentation and in tackle.

Boroughmuir couldn't have enjoyed a more encouraging launch to their campaign. In their first match they registered a record ten tries in crushing the champions of 1988 and 1989, Kelso, by 53-11. Indeed they scored 23 tries in their opening four games and yet hinted again at not putting the bits and pieces together against modest opposition when they required three penalty goals to squeeze through against newly-promoted Currie, who scored the only try through Grant Ferguson. It said a lot for Currie, who were coached by the former Boroughmuir and Scotland threequarter, Graham Hogg, that they survived for another season in Division One and played some attractive rugby in the process. Thereafter Boroughmuir's biggest problems were to be found in the Borders. At Netherdale Gala, with two tries to one, held them to an 18-18 draw, and at the Greenyards Jim Telfer's Melrose inflicted their only championship defeat by 13-10.

In the run-in, however, they still had to look to their laurels. Perhaps the game that convinced them that they had it in them to go all the way was that on February 23 at home against their old city rivals, Heriot's FP. A fortnight before that those two great clubs had lost their unbeaten championship records, Heriot's FP to Jed-Forest and Boroughmuir to Melrose, and it was obvious how tight a finish it was going to be.

Heriot's FP, coached by the former Hawick and Scotland lock, Iain Barnes, had come in for some flak for holding to a somewhat restricted format based around their heavy pack, the strength of a big scrum-half, Mike Allingham, and even more importantly the boot of the former Cambridge University blue, Cameron Glasgow. The critics felt that with a tradition for spreading the ball wide and with such a quick pivot player in Glasgow, Heriot's FP might have given it a twirl more often. Yet they could point to their pattern of play as having placed them in a strong championship challenging position. That is until they were outplayed by Boroughmuir to a tune of 24-7. By transforming their initial possession into fast ruck/maul delivery over the gain line and by intuitive interchange of duties as between the piano shifters and the piano players, Boroughmuir produced such a blend of drive and switch-play, in which the open-side flanker Drummond was here, there and everywhere, as to carry the day with a bit to spare. Not only that but, with a game in hand, they now had it in their own hands as to whether they won the title or not. They still had Edinburgh Academicals (away), Glasgow High-Kelvinside (away) and Edinburgh Wanderers (home) to play. Edinburgh Academicals had the same championship points as Boroughmuir 17; but on a wet day and sloppy pitch that were not conducive to the Academicals' natural flowing style, they still put up a gritty challenge before going down just 7-6. Even so Boroughmuir's try owed much to sharp opportunism and sweet interplay between forwards and backs – stand-off pirating loose ball, second five-eighth threatened further, open-side flanker and number 8 set up the delivery point and snappy service enabled the blind-side flanker to put the right wing in at the corner. GH-K were seen off, 23-15, partly because Murry Walker landed five penalty goals, and four backs and three forwards were the try-scorers in the 34-14 clincher against Edinburgh Wanderers.

In accepting the Division One trophy from the president of the SRU, Charlie Stewart of Kelso, Steve Douglas said that the players "had done it for Bruce after all the work he has put in". This was a deserved tribute to the coach, Bruce Hay, the former Lions full back and wing, who had set such a stirring example to his squad in dedication and commitment and in that ability to put previous disappointments behind him whilst also learning from them. Hay also had Scotland's Grand Slam captain of 1984, Jim Aitken, to help in preparing the forwards and that undoubtedly was an important factor in Boroughmuir's success.

Edinburgh had another reason for celebration in the feat of Watsonians in winning the Division Two title and so ensuring their return to the top flight for the coming season. Watsonians won all 13 games, produced the top try-scorer in the top two divisions in wing and captain Ian Smith with 13 (he scored 20 in all games) and had 149 of their 333 championship points from the inimitable Gavin Hastings who had brother Scott, and stand-off Andrew Ker, formerly of Kelso, as fellow internationalists in the back division. And to think that Roger Baird, now based in Edinburgh, is expected to play for Watsonians in the coming season as did his father Roger in the Fifties!

Sadly Kelso, for whom John Jeffrey turned down a Barbarians invitation in order to support his club in their relegation struggle, had the agony of waiting until the eleventh hour before hearing the unwelcome news that Stewart's-Melville FP, although beaten by Selkirk, 21-16, still finished the championship with a superior points differential so that Kelso were relegated to Division Two along with Edinburgh Wanderers.

Whilst the championship had a thrilling finish – at both ends – the standard of play was disappointing in that too many players went to ground preventing enough quick breakdown ball with which to ignite backs. There was a sad lack of continuity in action although it was encouraging that three clubs in particular who embraced an all-action, fluent style, Jed-Forest, Gala and Edinburgh Academicals, finished in the top half-dozen behind Boroughmuir and Heriot's FP.

There is no doubt, however, about who will be the team to beat when the 1991/92 National Leagues get under way on November 9. Not only did Boroughmuir win the Division One title but their understudies won the inter-city 2nd XV league with a 100% record over 13 games and their 3rds and youth sections have been going well too. Boroughmuir will open their title defence at home against young pretenders, Edinburgh Academicals, David Sole, John Allan, Alex Moore and all. Some opening!

Boroughmuir clinch the title with a win over Edinburgh Wanderers.

HEINEKEN LEAGUE EXAMINES WELSH CLUBS
by Lyn Davies

"Financially it's important that clubs like ourselves are very much involved in the Premier Division. It would probably mean financial ruin if we weren't in the top half of that league." Those were the pre-season words of Llanelli coach Gareth Jenkins – words that were quickly to haunt him as the Welsh Rugby Union at last put into motion its much discussed and opposed league system.

Llanelli promptly drew its first game against Pontypridd and then went down in its second to Abertillery to find itself at the bottom of the division. Indeed so many parts did the Heineken reach that Abertillery was immediately deemed team of the month; obviously the ad-man's claim that here was a brew more potent than any other had more substance to it than sheer fantasy.

Having grimaced at the first taste, Llanelli and others gradually acquired a taste for the fizz and pop and the extra competitive edge of this new concoction, and indeed for the men of Stradey Park it was to prove an integral part of a remarkable season! A season dominated by them and their arch rivals Neath, who at a canter won the inaugural Premier Division championship. Llanelli were winners, for the seventh time, of the Schweppes Cup.

Meetings between the two clubs were to prove high points in the season. Neath's early season league win at Stradey Park underlining that despite the loss to rugby league of three of its better players the machine rolled onward; sweeping less prepared, less committed opposition to one side. Laity's try from a sweeping 70 metres emphasized the point. The return at The Gnoll on the other hand saw Neath suffer their first league defeat; although it must be said that it wasn't quite contested on equal terms.

The week leading up to the game had been deemed one of preparation for the Welsh squad before the match against England. The endless slog of that week left the large Neath contingent completely drained and in no condition to have either the physical nor mental resolve to withstand the Llanelli onslaught.

The third and tie-breaking encounter between the two clubs came about under yet another set of experimental circumstances in the semi-final stage of the Schweppes Cup competition. The Welsh Rugby Union having deemed that both matches should be played on the same day, at the same venue – The National Stadium.

Here it was Llanelli's organizational ability and greater individual talent that won the day. Raising its game for the great occasion, especially at the National Stadium, has always been a special trait of the Scarlets and in the final against Pontypool it was seen at its best. Not that either game flowed but there was always enough tactical and confrontational edge around to satisfy most tastes.

Neath, having suffered early body blows in the loss of Allan Bateman, Roland Phillips and Mark Jones to rugby league can only look back on the season with a huge amount of pride. Indeed those losses may have strengthened the inner resolve, for its early season charge saw the half-way stage reached, in league title terms, unbeaten and uncatchable. That they were beaten more than once in the ensuing run-in speaks more of their own loss of concentration rather than great improvement elsewhere. The last four seasons have been ones of remarkably consistent success. That chapter however has now closed and it will be interesting to note how the new one opens under Neath's new chief executive Brian Thomas.

Outside of those top two clubs the rest of the Heineken League's Premier Division was afflicted with seemingly uncontrollable inconsistencies. How, for example, does one explain away Swansea? Multi-talented, with the ability not only to score breathtaking winning tries as was seen at Bridgend and to amass over 60 points against Pontypool, but then to finish perilously close to relegation and to be overwhelmed in the Cup semi-final by the very same men of Gwent.

Bridgend shadowed Neath for most the season but somehow could never release itself from the shackles of a rigid head-down approach, much to the chagrin of the likes of match-winning wing Glen Webbe. Pontypridd and Cardiff also had their odd moments. Luck may not have altogether favoured them, but the successful would claim that you make your own luck.

It was outside of that Premier Division though that the Heineken League was felt to its best effect. Mighty Newport made it plain that they were out of place in the First. A one season stay was more than enough, as the veterans Waters and Turner dominated their season. Waters provided the possession, Turner the points.

Whilst Newport's name is one from Welsh rugby's past, lower down there were new names emerging. Who could have envisaged an end of season promotion match between Dunvant and Llanharan – packed ground, TV outside broadcast and Trophy presentation? These two extremely well-organised clubs had tremendously successful seasons as did the promoted Third Division clubs Llandovery and Tenby. Indeed the whole competition changed the face of Welsh club rugby – yes the brew certainly reached the strangest of parts!

Mark Jones – here contesting a ball against Swansea – was just one of the Neath players lost to rugby league early in the season.

ENGLAND'S GRAND SLAM

TOP ROW
Left Mike Teague scores England's only try at Cardiff.
Left centre Another try for Teague against Ireland.
Right centre The England back row work as a team.
Right Dean Richards shadows Serge Blanco.
Far right Jeremy Guscott and Blanco contest a high ball.

MIDDLE ROW
Left and Centre Now you see him – now you don't. Rory Underwood leaves the Irish defence flat-footed to score a decisive try.
Right Underwood again – the only try against France.

BOTTOM ROW
Left Jeff Probyn goes down but Messrs Dooley and Ackford stand firm to hold the Scots.
Centre Will Carling leaves the field as Grand Slam captain.
Right Traditional celebrations.

The Whitbread *Rugby World* Annual Awards

Player of the Year	Dean Richards (Leicester)
International Player of the Year	Serge Blanco (Biarritz)
Senior Team of the Year	Orrell RFC
Most Promising Player	Simon Geoghegan (Hawick)
Junior Club of the Year	Tondu RFC
For Services to Rugby	Eric Smith
The Photograph of the Year	Hugh Routledge (The Times)
For Services to Journalism	Stephen Jones (Sunday Times)
Unsung Hero	The Wasps Front Row
Coach of the Year	Roger Uttley
Referee of the Year	Les Peard (Wales)
Youth Team of the Year	Wasps Colts
School of the Year	Merchiston Castle

Monthly Awards

November 1990

Senior Team   Wasps
Junior Team   Syston
Player   Stuart Barnes (Bath)
Heineken Welsh Team   Abertillery

December 1990

Senior Team   Wakefield
Junior Team   Thanet Wanderers
Player   Paul Thorburn (Neath)
Heineken Welsh Team   Dunvant

January 1990

Senior Team   Orrell
Junior Team   Old Halesonians
Player   Dean Richards (Leicester)
HeinekenWelsh Team   Tenby United

February 1991

Senior Team   Rugby
Junior Team   Ashbourne
Player   Mark Egan (Oxford University)
Heineken Welsh Team   Neath

March 1991

Senior Team   Llanelli
Junior Team   Bradford Salem
Player   Simon Hodgkinson (Nottingham)
Heineken Welsh Team   Llandovery

April 1991

Senior Team   Cork Constitution
Junior Team   Bicester
Player   Gary Armstrong (Jed-Forest)
Heineken Welsh Team   Aberavon Quins

May 1991

Senior Team   West Hartlepool
Junior Team   Towcestrians
Player   Jeff Probyn (Wasps)
Heineken Welsh Team   Newport

1. Orrell RFC.
2. The Wasps Front Row.
3. Eric Smith.
4. Serge Blanco.
5. Roger Uttley.
6. Stephen Jones.
7. Simon Geoghegan.
8. Hugh Routledge.
9. Master-in-charge Frank Hadden and captain James Scott, Merchiston Castle.
10. Les Peard.
11. Tondu RFC.
12. Coach Mike Clements, captain Paul Volley and president Charles O'Sullivan, Wasps Colts.

SERGE BLANCO

by Ian Robertson

When Mrs Blanco looked at the little bundle of joy born to her on 31st August, 1958 in Caracas, Venezuela, I don't suppose it crossed her mind that young Serge would one day become one of the greatest rugby players in the world.

Precious few sportsmen born in South America have ever reached the dizzy heights of international fame which Serge has enjoyed throughout a long and thrilling career. Precious few sporting personalities in France have won the hearts of the nation in the way Serge has since he won his first cap against South Africa in 1980.

He is the people's hero and in their eyes he has done, and can do, nothing wrong. He is a genius, a magician of a player; he is a unique and fabulous talent.

Serge Blanco with his wife.

For 12 marvellous and unforgettable seasons he has brought a tingling buzz of excitement whenever he is within reach of the ball, and so often in the heat of an international he has remained sublimely cool and ultra-confident as he has produced one miracle after another to prove that in his case the impossible is always possible, if not actually probable.

So often he has looked an artist sharing a pitch with 29 artisans. The ever-growing Blanco fan club would have you believe he can walk on water and I would certainly not want to bet against it. His colleague Frank Mesnel once said that other players pound or plod across the pitch but Serge Blanco glides over it. Mesnel said that on one occasion they played on a snow-covered pitch and when Blanco ran 50 yards to score his team-mates were not astonished to see that there were no Blanco footprints in the snow because he had simply floated over the ground.

What can one say about a multi-talented flamboyant sporting aristocrat who has achieved virtually everything in his glittering career? By the middle of 1991 he had played a world record number of 86 times for France and scored 34 tries as well as 21 penalties, 71 conversions and 2 drop goals. Only David Campese has scored more times in international rugby and no other player has reached 30 tries yet.

Blanco's breathtakingly refreshing approach has produced some of the very best and most lasting rugby memories of the past decade. His first thought

The would-be restaurateur surrounded by seafood from his home town of Biarritz.

is to attack, and so is his second, third and fourth thought. At Parc des Princes in 1991 the Welsh should not have been surprised when Blanco caught a wayward kick near his own '22' and decided to open out rather than clear his lines.

When challenged, he sprinted across the field to the open side and, still running flat out, he kicked ahead with deadly accuracy. He hurtled off in pursuit, seemingly turbo-charged and nuclear-powered, to hack the ball over the line with unerring precision and overtake the Welsh defence to score a spectacular try. The truth is that almost all of his 34 tries have been extra special because we are talking about an extra special player.

He had announced beforehand that the match against Wales was to be his final championship appearance in Paris. The crowd relished his try. He made another try for Lafond with his brilliant sense of timing by sucking the defence on to himself and releasing the unmarked Lafond at exactly the right moment. Ever the master showman, the old style theatrical actor/manager, he stole the final scene as only the star of the show could, by converting the last try from the touchline.

To exemplify his versatility and his genuine pace, he has won 12 caps on the wing as well as 74 at full back. This is not to suggest he could not have played fly-half or centre, because he most certainly could have. He is, without a shadow of a doubt, the complete all-round player. He has superb hands and a sharp eye although it is rumoured he once dropped a high ball in 1982. I refuse to believe it. Even if that particular match had been played under floodlights and there had been a power cut with the ball at its highest point, Serge would still not have dropped it. Not Serge. His kicking is long and accurate and he was raised at a time when players learned to use both feet. The fact that he missed very few games in 12 seasons is suitable testament to his fitness and training disciplines.

Of course other players have trained hard and could catch and kick. So what makes Serge so very special? I think there are several reasons. He has tremendous pace; he has a marvellous vision of the game; he has outrageous confidence to go with his outrageous talent – he manages to see a gap before the gap actually exists; and above all, he thinks big. Never for him the easy or safe option.

Regularly, he goes for broke and with his gloriously instinctive footballing ability he gets away with something no-one else would even have considered trying. Ballesteros has done it on the golf course and Viv Richards on the cricket field. Mere mortals set their sights a lot lower.

The final whistle went and as Serge moved off centre stage for the last time, to commemorate his final Five Nations match in Paris, he was presented with a magnificent statuette. Serge accepted it graciously and then jogged over to a young paralysed boy in a wheelchair on the touchline and gave him the statuette. The boy was overwhelmed. It was an overwhelming but typical Serge Blanco gesture.

That is the measure of the man and it is nice to think that this great player who can float imperiously over snow without leaving a footprint actually has both feet firmly on the ground. He well deserved his Oscar - Serge Blanco: Whitbread Rugby World 1991 International Player of the Year.

A SUMMARY OF THE SEASON
by Bill Mitchell

INTERNATIONAL RUGBY

NEW ZEALAND
IN FRANCE
OCTOBER – NOVEMBER 1990

Opponents	Results	
French Selection	L	15 – 19
Languedoc XV	W	22 – 6
Central France	W	27 – 24
French Barbarians	W	23 – 13
Cote Basque	L	12 – 15
FRANCE	W	24 – 3
France 'A'	W	22 – 15
FRANCE	W	30 – 12

Played 8 Won 6 Lost 2

ARGENTINA
IN THE BRITISH ISLES
OCTOBER – NOVEMBER 1990

Opponents	Results	
Ireland 'B'	L	12 – 27
Irish Students	W	23 – 6
IRELAND	L	18 – 20
Eastern Counties	W	28 – 15
ENGLAND	L	0 – 51
South of Scotland	W	13 – 10
SCOTLAND	L	3 – 49
Barbarians	L	22 – 34

Played 8 Won 3 Lost 5

SCOTLAND
IN NORTH AMERICA
MAY 1991

Opponents	Results	
BC President's XV	W	29 – 9
Alberta	W	76 – 7
Eastern United States	W	24 – 12
UNITED STATES	W	41 – 12
Ontario	W	43 – 3
CANADA	L	19 – 24

Played 6 Won 5 Lost 1

FRANCE
IN UNITED STATES
JULY 1991

Opponents	Results	
Western Selection	W	45 – 15
UNITED STATES	W	41 – 9
United States 'B'	W	61 – 6
UNITED STATES	W	10 – 3
(*abandoned due to lightning*)		

Played 4 Won 3 Abandoned 1

WALES
IN AUSTRALIA
JULY 1991

Opponents	Results	
West Australia	W	22 – 6
Queensland	L	24 – 35
ACT	W	7 – 3
New South Wales	L	8 – 71
Q'land Country District	W	35 – 7
AUSTRALIA	L	6 – 63

Played 6 Won 3 Lost 3

IRELAND
IN NAMIBIA
JULY 1991

Opponents	Results	
Namibia 'B'	W	45 – 16
NAMIBIA	L	6 – 15
Namibia South	W	35 – 4
NAMIBIA	L	15 – 26

Played 4 Won 2 Lost 2

Other International Tours

NAMIBIA
IN ENGLAND
OCT – NOV 1990

Opponents	Results	
Lancashire	W	23 – 15
England 'B'	L	16 – 31
Combined Services	W	16 – 13

Played 3 Won 2 Lost 1

ENGLAND
IN AUSTRALIA AND FIJI
MAY – JUNE 1990

Opponents	Results	
New South Wales	L	19 – 21
Victoria President's XV	W	26 – 9
Queensland	L	14 – 20
Fiji 'B'	L	13 – 27
FIJI	W	28 – 12
Emerging Wallabies	W	36 – 3
AUSTRALIA	L	15 – 40

Played 7 Won 3 Lost 4

EMERGING WALLABIES
IN ENGLAND
OCT – NOV 1990

Opponents	Results	
England Students	W	22 – 6
England 'B'	D	12 – 12

Played 2 Won 1 Drawn 1

Australian Schools
in Europe
December 1990– January 1991

Opponents	Results
NETHERLANDS	W 48–0
West Wales	W 32–7
East Wales	W 32–7
WALES	W 44–0
Leinster	W 23–13
Ulster	W 20–9
IRELAND	W 13–9
Munster	W 14–9
SCOTLAND	W 17–12
North & Midlands	Cancelled
London & South West	W 20–4
Harlequins Under 21	W 6–3
ENGLAND	W 8–3

Played 12 Won 12

Barbarians FC
Centenary Year
1990/91

Opponents	Results
ENGLAND	L 16–18
Bradford & Bingley	W 52–7
WALES	W 31–24
Newport	L 6–43
ARGENTINA	W 34–22
Leicester	W 26–21
East Midlands	W 46–34
Cardiff	W 42–25
Swansea	L 31–33

Played 9 Won 6 Lost 3

The Five Nations
Championship
1991

Results

France	15	Scotland	9
Wales	6	England	25
Ireland	13	France	21
Scotland	32	Wales	12
England	21	Scotland	12
Wales	21	Ireland	21
Ireland	7	England	16
France	36	Wales	3
Scotland	28	Ireland	25
England	21	France	19

	P	W	D	L	F	A	Pts
England	4	4	0	0	83	44	8
France	4	3	0	1	91	46	6
Scotland	4	2	0	2	81	73	4
Ireland	4	0	1	3	66	86	1
Wales	4	0	1	3	42	114	1

Other International Matches
Results

England U 21	16	Ireland U 21	22
Spain	7	Scotland 'A'	39
Ireland 'B'	16	Scotland 'B'	0
England 'B'	50	Spain	6
Ireland 'B'	24	England 'B'	10
Italy	9	France 'A'	15
Scotland 'B'	10	France 'B'	31
England 'B'	6	France 'B'	10
England 'B'	12	Italy 'B'	9
Romania	18	Italy	21
Netherlands	12	Wales 'B'	34

Bledisloe Cup

Australia	21	New Zealand	12
New Zealand	6	Australia	3

CLUB, COUNTY AND DIVISIONAL RUGBY

ENGLAND

Pilkington Cup
Quarter-finals

Harlequins	24	Bath	12
Northampton	10	Moseley	6
Nottingham	46	London Irish	9
Wasps	9	Orrell	15

Semi-finals

Harlequins	22	Nottingham	18
Northampton	18	Orrell	10

Final

Harlequins	25	Northampton	13

(after extra time)

Courage Leagues
Division One

	P	W	D	L	F	A	Pts
Bath	12	11	0	1	280	104	22
Wasps	12	9	1	2	252	151	19
Harlequins	12	8	0	4	267	162	16
Leicester	12	8	0	5	244	140	16
Orrell	12	7	0	5	247	105	14
Gloucester	12	6	0	6	207	163	12
Rosslyn Park	12	6	0	6	216	174	12
Nottingham	12	6	0	6	149	254	11
Saracens	12	5	0	7	151	228	10
Bristol	12	4	1	7	135	219	9
Moseley	12	1	1	10	113	244	3
L'pool St H	12	0	0	12	88	349	0

Division Two

	P	W	D	L	F	A	Pts
Rugby	12	10	0	2	252	146	20
London Irish	12	9	1	2	239	192	19
Wakefield	12	8	0	4	188	109	16
Coventry	12	8	0	4	240	178	16
N-Gosforth	12	6	0	5	169	140	12
Sale	12	5	1	6	224	156	11
Bedford	12	4	2	6	138	203	10
Waterloo	12	4	1	7	154	206	9
Blackheath	12	4	0	8	134	169	8
Plymouth	12	4	0	8	129	210	8
Richmond	12	3	1	8	134	245	7
Headingley	12	3	0	9	125	215	6

Division Three Champions: West Hartlepool
Runners-up: Morley
Division Four North: Otley
Division Four South: Redruth

ADT County Championship
Semi-finals

Yorkshire	14	Middlesex	0
Cornwall	14	Warwickshire	6

Final

Cornwall	29	Yorkshire	20

(after extra time)

ADT Divisional Championship

	P	W	D	L	F	A	Pts
London	3	2	1	0	80	44	5
Midlands	3	1	1	1	73	49	3
South West	3	0	2	1	21	46	2
North	3	0	2	1	23	58	2

Provincial Insurance Cup Final

Bicester	12	Bradford Salem	17

University Match

Oxford Univ	21	Cambridge Univ	12

University Under 21 Match

Oxford Univ	21	Cambridge Univ	16

UAU Cup Final

Cardiff	14	Swansea	3

BPSA (Polytechnics) Cup Final

Newcastle	20	Oxford	9

British Colleges Cup Final

Cardiff IHE	47	W London IHE	12

Students League Cup Final

Bristol Univ	31	W London IHE	12

Hospitals Cup

St Mary's	15	London	8

Inter-Services Champions: RAF
Middlesex Sevens Champions: L Scottish
National Sevens Champions: Bath

WALES

SCOTLAND

Schweppes Welsh Challenge Cup
Quarter-finals

Bridgend	10	Llanelli	16
Neath	16	Cardiff	13
Pontypool	12	Newbridge	3
Swansea	22	Tondu	13

Semi-finals

Pontypool	28	Swansea	10
Llanelli	22	Neath	10

Final

Llanelli	24	Pontypool	9

Heineken Leagues
Premier Division

	P	W	D	L	F	A	Pts
Neath	18	14	0	4	353	218	28
Llanelli	18	12	1	5	409	292	25
Bridgend	18	10	2	6	288	275	22
Cardiff	18	10	1	7	396	261	21
Pontypridd	18	9	2	7	353	270	20
Pontypool	18	9	1	8	402	293	19
Newbridge	18	9	0	9	363	261	18
Swansea	18	9	0	9	353	309	18
Glam Wdrs	18	3	0	15	192	496	6
Abertillery	18	1	1	16	146	580	3

First Division

	P	W	D	L	F	A	Pts
Newport	14	13	0	1	499	101	26
Maesteg	14	10	0	4	299	158	20
S W Police	14	10	0	4	262	161	20
Aberavon	14	8	0	6	275	191	16
Cross Keys	14	7	0	7	209	182	14
Ebbw Vale	14	4	0	10	183	348	8
Tredegar	14	4	0	10	117	265	8
Penarth	14	0	0	14	73	511	0

Second Division Champions: Dunvant
Runners-up: Llanharan
Third Division Champions: Llandovery
Runners-up: Tenby United

McEwans Inter-District Championship

	P	W	D	L	F	A	Pts
South	4	3	1	0	103	42	7
Glasgow	4	2	1	1	52	57	5
Edinburgh	4	1	2	1	61	68	4
Anglo Scots	4	1	0	3	35	55	2
N. & Midlands	4	1	0	3	48	77	2

McEwans National Leagues
Division One

	P	W	D	L	F	A	Pts
Boroughmuir	13	11	1	1	285	124	23
Heriots FP	13	11	0	2	276	144	22
Jed-Forest	13	10	0	3	268	166	20
Gala	13	9	1	2	271	167	19
Melrose	13	9	0	4	195	155	18
Edinb'gh Ac	13	8	1	4	270	139	17
Stirling Co	13	6	2	5	191	191	14
Hawick	13	6	0	7	207	191	12
Selkirk	13	5	0	8	184	276	10
Currie	13	3	1	9	200	268	7
Stew/Mel FP	13	3	0	10	166	236	6
G'gow High/K	13	3	0	10	170	264	6
Kelso	13	3	0	10	209	312	6
Edinb'gh W	13	1	0	12	144	403	2

Division Two

	P	W	D	L	F	A	Pts
Watsonians	13	13	0	0	333	79	26
W of Scotl'd	13	11	0	2	389	164	22
Dundee HS FP	13	10	0	3	338	159	20
Ayr	13	8	0	5	237	155	16
Glasgow Ac	13	7	1	5	220	232	15
Kirkcaldy	13	6	1	6	182	222	13
Kilmarnock	13	5	1	7	148	229	11
Corstorphine	13	5	1	7	203	307	11
Preston L FP	13	4	1	8	144	200	9
Royal High	13	4	1	8	155	246	9
Dunfermline	13	4	0	9	172	208	8
Musselburgh	13	4	0	9	178	236	8
H'head/J'hill	13	3	2	8	150	232	8
Langholm	13	2	2	9	107	287	6

Division Three Champions: Peebles
Runners-up: Wigtownshire
Division Four Champions: Dumfries
Runners-up: Hutchesons/Aloysians

IRELAND

All-Ireland Leagues

Division One

	P	W	D	L	F	A	Pts
Cork Const	8	7	0	1	119	78	14
Garryowen	8	6	0	2	120	76	12
Lansdowne	8	6	0	2	133	99	12
Shannon	8	5	0	3	108	99	10
Ballymena	8	3	1	4	113	115	7
Instonians	8	3	1	4	99	116	7
St Mary's Coll	8	2	0	6	91	106	4
Wanderers	8	2	0	6	83	112	4
Malone	8	1	0	7	80	145	2

Division Two

Old Wesley	9	8	0	1	143	72	16
Young M'ster	9	6	2	1	127	67	14
Bangor	9	6	1	2	154	101	13
Terenure Coll	9	6	0	3	174	70	12
Greystones	9	5	0	4	146	91	10
Sunday's Well	9	4	1	4	103	71	9
CIYMS	9	4	1	4	129	111	9
NIFC	9	2	0	7	90	166	4
Athlone	9	1	1	7	55	190	3
Corinthians	9	0	0	9	46	228	0

Inter-Provincial Championship

	P	W	D	L	F	A	Pts
Ulster	3	3	0	0	48	30	6
Munster	3	2	0	1	61	49	4
Leinster	3	1	0	2	38	58	2
Connacht	3	0	0	3	45	55	0

Senior Provincial Cup Finals

Leinster:
Lansdowne 13 Terenure College 9
Munster:
Shannon 15 Young Munster 9
Ulster:
Ballymena 13 Bangor 0
Connacht:
Athlone 10 Galwegians 9

FRANCE

French Club Championship
Semi-finals
Bègles-Bordeaux 13 Béziers 12
Toulouse 13 Racing Club 12
Final
Bègles-Bordeaux 19 Toulouse 10